Mercosur

MERCOSUR

Regional Integration, World Markets

edited by

Riordan Roett

LYNNE
RIENNER
PUBLISHERS

BOULDER
LONDON

Published in the United States of America in 1999 by
Lynne Rienner Publishers, Inc.
1800 30th Street, Boulder, Colorado 80301

and in the United Kingdom by
Lynne Rienner Publishers, Inc.
3 Henrietta Street, Covent Garden, London WC2E 8LU

Library of Congress Cataloging-in-Publication Data
Mercosur : regional integration, world markets / edited by Riordan
 Roett.
  p. cm.
  Includes bibliographical references and index.
  ISBN 1-55587-837-7 (hardcover : alk. paper).—ISBN 1-55587-838-5
(pbk. : alk. paper)
   1. MERCOSUR (Organization) 2. South America—Economic
integration. 3. South America—Commerce. I. Roett, Riordan, 1938– .
HC165.M4569   1999
337.1'8—dc21   98-37779
                                                                CIP

British Cataloguing in Publication Data
A Cataloguing in Publication record for this book
is available from the British Library.

Printed and bound in the United States of America

     The paper used in this publication meets the requirements
 ∞ of the American National Standard for Permanence of
     Paper for Printed Library Materials Z39.48-1984.

5 4 3 2 1

Contents

Tables

Foreword

Mercosur has become an important regional actor in the Southern Cone of Latin America. The still-evolving customs union formed by four countries—Argentina, Brazil, Paraguay, and Uruguay—plus two associate members—Bolivia and Chile—may yet expand to include other countries in the region. Mercosur's dynamism raises critical policy questions regarding the process of building a Free Trade Area of the Americas, an initiative proposed by the United States in 1994. The controversy over the issue of hemispheric integration underscores the divergence between the broad U.S. approach, which seeks to use the North American Free Trade Agreement as a model for creating a Free Trade Area of the Americas by the year 2005, and the slower, incremental approach advocated by the countries of Mercosur.

Mercosur has already created significant new trade flows both within the member countries and externally, particularly with the European Union and with other Latin American countries. Another important element that has emerged from the economic integration process is Mercosur's role in the consolidation of democratic institutions in the region.

This volume provides a comprehensive review of the origins, current status, and future evolution of Mercosur. In the first chapters the authors provide a historical overview of Mercosur; they explain the importance of Brazil—the largest economy of Mercosur—and its powerful negotiating position within the bloc; and they explore the complexities of reconciling the domestic and foreign policy goals of the member countries, particularly Argentina and Brazil, with trade negotiations and the process of economic integration. The discussion then turns to some of the most pressing issues that Mercosur countries must resolve: finding the right balance between "broadening" and "deepening" the trade arrangement and finding a regional approach to an industrial policy that will make Mercosur more competitive. The final chapters deal with Mercosur's external trade negotiations, the evolving biregional relationship between Mercosur and the European Union, and the U.S. approach to Mercosur and hemispheric integration.

This volume is the culmination of a one-year project on Mercosur that marks the first phase of a broader SAIS program on regional integration in the Western Hemisphere. The project was carried out with the support of the William and Flora Hewlett Foundation. Other SAIS publications completed with the Hewlett Foundation's support include *Mexico's Private Sector: Recent History, Future Challenges* (1998), *The Mexican Peso Crisis: International Perspectives* (1996), *The Challenge of Institutional Reform in Mexico* (1995), *Political and Economic Liberalization in Mexico: At a Critical Juncture?* (1993), *Mexico's External Relations in the 1990s* (1991), and *Mexico and the United States: Managing the Relationship* (1988).

Guadalupe Paz
Assistant Director
SAIS Latin American Studies Program

Acknowledgments

I owe my sincere gratitude to the authors of this volume, whose commitment and time dedicated to this project went far beyond what was initially requested of them. Others who deserve special acknowledgment for their valuable work are Guadalupe Paz, the program's assistant director, for coordinating the project and overseeing every step in the editing and publication process; Donna Verdier for her superb editing work; and Charles Roberts for his able translation work.

My deepest gratitude goes to Clint Smith and the Hewlett Foundation for making it possible to continue our efforts to contribute to the field of Latin American studies.

Riordan Roett

Introduction

Riordan Roett

Today it is widely accepted that free markets and democracy are important components of Latin America's strategy for achieving economic and political consolidation. Indeed, efforts such as the Mercosur agreement,[1] the topic of this book, are definitive signs that Latin America (the Southern Cone countries in particular) is progressing along this still-uncertain path. What is often overlooked, however, is that only recently did many of these countries emerge from a long period of military dictatorships and statist economic policies. And since it is generally agreed that economic reform and integration help bolster democracy, it is arguable that Mercosur's political impact will be as great as—if not greater than—its economic benefits. As recently as the 1980s, Brazil and Argentina were uneasy neighbors, each believing that it was locked in a zero-sum game to determine which country would be the dominant player in the region. Today, old antagonisms have receded, and the countries of Mercosur are in the process of creating a challenging and complex set of relationships. It is within this new framework that we will analyze the evolution of Mercosur as well as its present challenges and future prospects.

The long history of failed efforts to integrate the South American nation-states led many observers to underestimate the determination of the Mercosur partners to succeed in consolidating their customs union. A Latin American Free Trade Association (LAFTA) in 1960 had failed; its successor, the Latin American Integration Association (ALADI), although somewhat more focused, did not accomplish the goal of initiating a dynamic process of regional integration. Finally, in 1991, driven by a shared belief that economic integration and harmonization was the best way to push forward the process of regional economic stabilization and ultimately to end the cycle of hyperinflation and economic mismanagement, Mercosur came into existence with the Treaty of Asunción. This accord formally joined Argentina and Brazil with Paraguay and Uruguay in an ambitious undertaking to create a customs union in South America. Trade, although always the most visible component of any agreement such as Mercosur, is only one of the many facets of the experiment begun in Asunción in 1991. Much remains to be accomplished before we can be confident that the agreement will grow and mature into a fully integrated customs union in the next decade.

Because the contemporary global economy is replete with high-quality, low-cost producers, it is vital that the countries of Mercosur maximize their competitiveness, primarily by striving to create dynamic comparative advantages. Thus, a strategic industrial policy is inevitable. Within this context, it will be essential for the Mercosur countries to promote export sectors whose products have high technological content so as to reap the greatest possible benefits from increased trade.

Linked directly to the expansion of trade opportunities is the important question of when and how Mercosur should "broaden" by adding new members and "deepen" by creating an institutional infrastructure that can, for example, facilitate further trade integration and direct foreign investment and quickly resolve disputes among the members and associates. The decisions needed in both areas are essentially of a political nature and will respond to the rhythm of elections and internal dynamics in each of the member states in the years ahead.

Mercosur's dynamism is probably best seen in the ambitious efforts to promote its external trade relations with other Latin American countries as well as with other regions of the world. Already, two countries (Chile and Bolivia) have gained associate member status, and there is talk of eventually adding some or all of the other countries of the Andean region.[2] But, most important, the success of Mercosur has given it the ability to negotiate any upcoming trade agreements from a position of strength and solidarity. Thus, if either the European Union or North American countries want to sign an agreement, they will have to treat Mercosur as an equal partner— they cannot simply dictate the terms of the agreement.

Following the Summit of the Americas in Santiago in April 1998, a long process of hemisphere-wide trade negotiations began, whereby the framework for an eventual free trade pact will be ironed out. Mercosur is fully prepared to participate, but only on an equal footing with North America. Efforts made before the Santiago meetings to address the agenda of North America—or, more precisely, the United States—were rebuffed by Brazil and the other countries in South America. Their position was simple and direct: The Free Trade Area of the Americas (FTAA) negotiations will be an open process in which Mercosur and other subregional groupings will receive their full due.

A number of other important economic and political issues since 1991 have colored the growth and development of Mercosur. Many of these matters have been either overlooked or taken lightly by those who see Mercosur as an overly ambitious attempt to create a common market in a region with a less than stellar track record in cooperation or burden sharing. Nevertheless, these issues have had a direct impact on the path taken by the member states in structuring the emerging, though imperfect, common market of South America.

The first, and for many observers the most surprising, step along that path was the dramatic turnabout in relations between Argentina and Brazil, the core states of Mercosur. After 150 years of suspicion and rivalry, a fundamental shift occurred in the late 1980s and 1990s with the end of military dictatorships and the installation of elected civilian regimes. For the political leadership of both countries, the decision to seek new levels of regional integration was fundamental in securing the fragile democratic regimes. Although technically the transitions occurred in 1983 in Argentina and in 1985 in Brazil, the successor governments were weak and unable to undertake fundamental structural reforms. Only with the second—in the case of Brazil, the third—transitional regime was it feasible to use the political legitimacy bestowed with a popular electoral mandate to begin to fashion a different economic future. Quickly, Argentina and Brazil identified regional economic cooperation as a major component of the process of internal economic and financial reform.

As part of this deepening of regional cooperation, Argentina and Brazil have taken a number of steps in the field of security and geopolitics. In November 1990 both states agreed to ban nuclear weapons and to accede to the international nuclear proliferation agreements in force. Moreover, both states agreed to create a "strategic alliance" in 1997 with the Rio Declaration, an accord that commits them to joint military consultations and creation of a broad agenda to preclude regional military adventurism. Yet, not surprisingly, the two countries still have their differences. It is not clear which of the two will be a candidate for a Latin American seat on the United Nations Security Council, and this competition has kept alive a semblance of the old regional rivalry. Few doubt that such differences will continue, but none of these is expected to derail what has become an important new sense of diplomatic purpose and collaboration in both capitals.

Another development unforeseen in the early planning years was the sudden initiative of the Clinton administration in 1994 to unilaterally call for a Summit of the Americas. That summit, held in Miami in December 1994, called for the expansion of the North American Free Trade Agreement (NAFTA) to include Chile and for the creation of a hemisphere-wide FTAA by 2005. But, without warning, several events stymied achievement of President Clinton's goal. The Mexican peso crisis of December 1994 and the ensuing "tequila effect" adversely affected most Latin

American economies and turned many against further free trade initiatives. Many pundits predicted that this anti–free trade sentiment would cause leaders in the Southern Cone to lose their will to continue the integration process, causing Mercosur to quickly come unraveled. Fortunately, this did not happen. If anything, the economic difficulties stemming from the Mexican crisis just served to reinforce the region's commitment to Mercosur. A good indicator of this resolve was that not one part of the Mercosur framework was nullified or even delayed throughout this time of economic strife. It therefore comes as little surprise that during the Asian economic crisis of 1997 and 1998 and the subsequent "flu" that affected Latin American economies, virtually no one was predicting the disintegration of Mercosur.

The Mercosur countries' dedication to staying solidly on the path of regional integration has paralleled an important development outside the region—the growing interest of the European Union (EU) in strengthening and broadening its contacts with South America. The dialogue, which has addressed social and political matters as well as the obvious trade and investment goals, has produced an interregional cooperation framework agreement (December 1995) and will result in a Mercosur-EU summit in Brazil in 1999. The longer-term goal is a free trade agreement between the two groups in 2006. The EU's interest in Mercosur is obvious. History, language, and culture provide the rationale for ties with the countries of the region, and from the South American perspective, the overall relationship has been richer and deeper than the dialogue with the United States, which narrowly focuses on trade concessions.

Mercosur is an imaginative and bold initiative that has laid to rest the traditional diplomatic rivalries and spasmodic conflicts that afflicted the region. Nevertheless, many trade, investment, and institutional issues need to be addressed, and there is no guarantee that they will be dealt with successfully. The possibility of broadening—full membership for Chile and Bolivia as well as possible associate affiliation for other Andean countries—helps set the agenda for the next century, and the working relationship with the European Union offers a useful route for escaping the rigid and outdated security relationship with the United States.

South America is changing, and Mercosur is a concrete manifestation of that fact. It is now time for North America to come to terms with that change, and the ongoing negotiations for an FTAA are an important venue for doing so. North America should keep firmly in mind that those negotiations will take place in the shadow of Mercosur's emerging relationship with the EU and other regions of the world as well as within the spirit of the new democratic political realities of the countries of the Southern Cone.

NOTES

1. *Mercosur,* which stands for Mercado Común del Sur (Common Market of the South), is the most widely used acronym, but the agreement is also known as *Mercosul,* the Portuguese equivalent of the Spanish acronym.

2. Bolivia, a member of the Andean Pact, obtained special authorization from its Andean partners to negotiate an accord with Mercosur.

1

Toward the Common Market of the South: Mercosur's Origins, Evolution, and Challenges

Lia Valls Pereira

On March 26, 1991, the presidents of Argentina, Brazil, Paraguay, and Uruguay signed the Treaty of Asunción, with a view to forming the Common Market of the South (Mercosur).[1] The free circulation of goods, services, and factors of production among the member countries, characteristic of the formation of a common market, was provided for in the treaty, which was to go into force on January 1, 1995.

The goal of implementing the common market was not met in the anticipated time frame. Recalling, however, the not-so-successful results of previous plans for integrating Latin America, Mercosur has fared well indeed: The share of intraregional trade in the total exports of Mercosur countries increased from 8 to 21 percent between 1991 and 1996, accompanied by greater cooperation among firms in the establishment of subsidiaries and joint ventures as well as by stepped-up purchase of equity shares within the region. The Code of Common Safeguards regarding imports from third countries was adopted, as were Common Investment Protocols. Both Chile and Bolivia entered into free trade agreements with Mercosur.

Still pending, however, is a vast agenda for implementing a common market. In addition, the extremely asymmetrical nature of the integration effort—a single country, Brazil, accounts for about 70 percent of Mercosur's gross domestic product (GDP)—raises questions about the prospects for thoroughgoing integration. Also in question is the priority the member countries accord to their respective economic stabilization plans. Given these issues, there is still controversy over the best way to consolidate Mercosur.

In this chapter I give an overview of the historical antecedents to

7

Mercosur, describe the institutional evolution of Mercosur and the major developments that have shaped the integration process, and take up some of the basic issues that permeate the debate on the future of Mercosur; conclusions are presented in the last section.

HISTORICAL BACKGROUND

Integration agreements aimed at creating free trade areas, customs unions, or common markets are not new in Latin America, but they have lacked the strong base necessary to reach their goal. Issues of macroeconomic stability, border disputes, and protectionist trade policies explain in part the weak bases of those proposals for integration.

In 1960 the Latin American Free Trade Association (LAFTA) was created with a view to forming a free trade area within twelve years. LAFTA was based on the idea that the integration project, by expanding the market, would prove positive for the import-substitution model through gains in economy of scale. However, the inherent contradiction between the idea of giving impetus to integration via trade liberalization and the protectionist logic of the import-substitution model did not provide a favorable context for integration. The governments were accustomed to thinking of protectionism as a stimulus to growth, and so were reluctant to offer long lists of goods for liberalization.

The recognition of LAFTA's scant results led to the creation of the Latin American Integration Association (Asociación Latinoamericana de Integración, or ALADI) in 1980. ALADI did not establish rigid time lines for the formation of a free trade area, nor did it even set up automatic instruments to eliminate trade barriers among the member countries. The objective was simply to arrange preferential tariff agreements among the member countries that desired them. The ideal of a free trade area was maintained, but it would supposedly be achieved as the countries extended their preferential agreements.

During that same period, in late 1979, diplomatic relations between Brazil and Argentina began to thaw with the signing of the tripartite agreement among Argentina, Brazil, and Paraguay. That agreement made it possible to solve the dispute regarding the use of border water resources, which had undermined relations between Argentina and Brazil in the 1970s.

Improved diplomatic relations, however, were not immediately followed by efforts to deepen economic relations. The 1982 foreign debt crisis led to the erection of new protectionist barriers in many Latin American countries, including Brazil, and the resulting climate was not favorable to economic integration projects. Nevertheless, the process of redemocratization in Argentina and Brazil in the mid-1980s brought these two countries' experiences into even closer alignment, which was officially recognized in 1986 with the signing of the Program for Integration and Economic Cooperation (PICE).

The PICE was structured around the negotiation of sectoral agreements covering such areas as capital goods, food, technological cooperation, and the iron, steel, nuclear, and auto industries, among others. The conception of sectoral integration addressed two concerns. First, it reflected an interest in planning and consolidating the industrial process.[2] Second, the emphasis on achieving balanced trade between the sectors of the two countries helped attenuate the fears of both Argentine and Brazilian businesses regarding possible losses.

The worldwide trend toward regionalization, the notion that Latin American countries were outside the area of economic interest to the developed countries, and the choice to open trade in Brazil and Argentina explain the signing of the Treaty on Integration, Cooperation, and Development in November 1988.[3] It was aimed at forming a common market within ten years. Later, in late 1990, the presidents of Brazil and Argentina signed the Act of Buenos Aires, which anticipated that the common market would come into effect in 1995. Finally, the Treaty of Asunción was signed in March 1991, bringing in Paraguay and Uruguay and creating Mercosur.

The change in the format of the integration process, from sectoral agreements to wide-ranging liberalization, is largely explained by national objectives. Trade or other economic ties, by themselves, cannot account for the change in approach. From 1986 to 1991, there was no significant increase in trade that would have suggested the formation of a free trade area. Instead, in the late 1980s Argentina, and later Brazil, came to adopt liberal economic policy guidelines, according priority to the market as a mechanism for fostering efficiency. The liberalization of intraregional trade reinforces the commitment to such a policy. Mercosur was a political initiative of the governments of Brazil and Argentina made in part to consolidate their economic direction as well as to respond to the trend toward regionalization of the global economy.

THE INSTITUTIONAL EVOLUTION OF MERCOSUR

The customs union of the Mercosur countries was created on January 1, 1995, although it will not enter into force as a true customs union, with completely free intraregional trade among all its member countries and a uniform common external tariff, until 2006. This section covers first the years 1991–1994, during which the negotiations that led to the formation of the customs union were conducted, and then developments since 1995, when issues of deepening integration in the direction of a common market emerged.

The Treaty of Asunción

The main provisions of the Treaty of Asunción of March 26, 1991, out of which Mercosur was born, may be summarized as follows.

First, the treaty listed four instruments for forming the common market: the trade liberalization program, the common external tariff, the coordination of macroeconomic policy, and the adoption of sectoral agreements. With the exception of the intraregional trade liberalization programs, however, there was no guidance about how the instruments should be implemented.

Second, the institutional structure during the transition period, which was to run until December 31, 1994, was spelled out. Article 18 required that the "states parties" meet before that date to decide on the definitive structure of the common market. During the transition period intergovernmental organs were established, with decisions made by consensus. Therefore, whether measures agreed upon during the negotiating process were adopted depended on the national governments.

The organizational structure in the transition period comprised the Common Market Council (CMC) and the Common Market Group (Grupo Mercado Común, or GMC). The CMC, composed of the ministers of foreign affairs and economy of the member countries, was the highest-ranking body, responsible for the political direction of the integration process. The GMC was the implementing organ, coordinated by the ministries of foreign affairs and made up of representatives of public entities of the national governments. Working subgroups were created under the GMC to address the instruments required to form the common market.[4]

Third, the treaty contained four annexes that further delineated Mercosur practices. Annex 1 specified the program for tariff reduction in intraregional trade, with quantitative goals to be met in each six-month period until full free trade was attained; the date set for full free trade was December 31, 1994, for Argentina and Brazil, and one year later for Paraguay and Uruguay. The different timetables for the member countries accommodated a list of exceptions (that is, goods not subject to the parameters of the general tariff reduction process) allowed in recognition that the smaller economies would require more time in the adjustment process for goods deemed sensitive.[5] The other annexes addressed rules of origin, dispute settlement, and the formation of the working subgroups of the GMC.[6]

In essence, then, the Treaty of Asunción defined the implementation of automatic tariff reductions among the member countries, beginning as of the date of its signing. Arriving at guidelines for negotiating all the other issues that needed to be worked out to form the common market would be the task of the intergovernmental entities created by the treaty. From this perspective, the only supranational instrument to which all of the member countries were subordinated was the liberalization of intraregional trade.

Results of the Transition Period, 1991–1994

The Protocol of Ouro Preto, dated December 17, 1994, marked the end of the transition period and implementation of the main results negotiated during that period.

In the institutional realm there were few changes, except that Mercosur came to have international juridical personality, which enables it to participate as a single entity in international negotiations. As for the existing organs, the Common Market Council and Common Market Group remain, with essentially the same functions they had earlier.[7] The Commission on Trade was created and entrusted with implementing and monitoring the instruments for common trade policy; the technical committees for addressing the relevant matters in this area are organized under it.[8] The commission is also to conduct preliminary technical reviews of complaints lodged by member countries on breaches of the rules on common trade policy. Like the GMC and the CMC, the Commission on Trade is an intergovernmental body. The Joint Parliamentary Commission, made up of legislators from the four countries, and the Advisory Forum on Economic and Social Matters with representatives from business and labor, were also created. Neither body has decisionmaking power, but each is responsible for monitoring and making recommendations concerning the integration process.

The customs union, which came into force on January 1, 1995 (with the full customs union to take effect in 2006), listed some exceptions that took into account the different productive structures of the member countries. First are exceptions to the common external tariff in the capital goods, computer, and telecommunications sectors, which respond to these sectors' development in Argentina and Brazil.[9]

During the negotiations Argentina had zero tariffs on capital goods and computer goods, because the country did not produce computer goods, and the value added to capital goods had fallen from 23.14 percent in 1985 to 17.7 percent in 1990.[10] Argentina's strategy after the 1980s therefore was to eliminate import tariffs and protect domestic industry—the importation of capital goods at international prices was thought to be an effective vehicle for accelerating the modernization of Argentine industrial capacity. Brazil, however, as the sole producer of computers and the largest producer of capital goods in Mercosur, was not willing to agree on a zero tariff for these goods. Keeping tariffs in place in these sectors, which had long benefited from protectionist policies, seemed justified by the relatively large and diversified stock of capital goods and by some potentially competitive segments of the computer industry. The cost of adopting zero tariffs would have been extremely high. The solution was to delay implementation of the common external tariff. An average tariff of 14 percent will go into effect for capital goods in 2001; for computer goods and telecommunications, the average tariff will be 16 percent as of 2006.

The second group of exceptions refers to intraregional trade. Adjustment lists, which encompass a limited number of products that fall outside the intraregional free trade regime, will expire on January 1, 1999, for Brazil and Argentina, and one year later for Paraguay and Uruguay. In addition, the automotive and sugar sectors are subject to special agreements under the Protocol of Ouro Preto; a common policy will be adopted by the year 2000 for Brazil and Argentina and 2001 for Paraguay and Uruguay. Notwithstanding these exceptions, some 88 percent of the goods on which tariffs are levied came under the common external tariff as of January 1, 1995.

Two agreements concerning investment were also signed during the transition period. The Protocol of Colonia del Sacramento, Uruguay, for the Promotion and Mutual Protection of Investments in Mercosur (December 1993) ensured national treatment for investment in the region.[11] In addition, performance requirements on investments were prohibited, and rules were laid down regarding compensation in the event of expropriation. The exceptions to the agreement reflect the status of pertinent regulations in each country; Brazil submitted the longest list. The Protocol on Promotion of Investments from States Not Members of Mercosur (August 1994) addressed third-country investments. It guarantees the right of each member country to promote and admit external investment, pursuant to its national legislation. It also lays down provisions for fair treatment of foreign capital. Both of these protocols provide for dispute settlement through consultation, recourse to a court with jurisdiction in the member country in which the investment was made, or, as a last resort, arbitration panels. The protocols do not aim to establish an all-encompassing discipline common to the countries of Mercosur; rather, they can best be understood as defining a conceptual framework, setting out guidelines for actions that are not allowed.[12]

As measured against the goal of forming the common market, the transition period produced scant results for the implementation of common policies, regulations, and institutions. Nonetheless, considering the relatively fragile ties of interdependence and the economic asymmetries among the member countries, the program for removing tariff barriers in intraregional trade and the customs union, with timetables defined for the sensitive sectors, constitute an important step along the road to integration.

During the years in which the negotiations were undertaken (1991–

1994), Argentina and Brazil, the partners with the greatest political and economic weight in Mercosur, were experiencing different economic conditions and therefore were responding to the challenge to restructure the state at distinct paces and in different ways. From 1991 to 1994 the Argentine economy consistently had positive, relatively high rates of economic growth, whereas the Brazilian economy saw either negative growth or positive growth at rates lower than in Argentina.[13] In addition, Argentina's exchange rate policy of parity with the dollar, in contrast to Brazil's policy of adjusting the exchange rate to account for inflation—which ran as high as 2,000 percent in 1993 and 1994—was extremely favorable for Brazilian exports. The real rate of exchange between the Brazilian and Argentine currencies reached 155.6 in December 1993, using a March 1991 baseline. The two countries' asynchronous macroeconomic cycles translated into an accumulation of surpluses with Argentina; in 1993 the balance of trade between Brazil and Argentina was positive, at U.S.$1.03 billion.

These asymmetries gave rise to tensions, as was to be expected. Argentina on several occasions called for safeguard clauses and thirteen times applied antidumping duties to Brazilian imports, and the private sector entered into agreements for the purpose of "putting order into the market," especially with respect to paper, steel, textiles, and apparel. These tensions could have been avoided, in principle, by having community policies on compensation or industrial conversion, or both. Yet as Bouzas has noted, this dynamic kept the integration process from being blocked by the sheer amount of resources that would have to have been spent on the costs of adjustment.[14] The negative side, according to the same author, is that in the absence of any clear agreement on a frame of reference, a climate of uncertainty set in as responsibility for dealing with conflictual situations fell to the national governments.

Several issues were pending on the wide-ranging negotiating agenda for various reasons, but especially because of reforms in Brazil. For example, the question of the liberalization of services depended on congressional approval in the area of telecommunications. The preference for placing priority on trade-related issues from 1991 to 1994 can be understood as a response to integration. The increase in intraregional trade from 8 percent in 1991 to 19 percent in 1994 suggested Mercosur's potential. In particular, for Brazil—the largest economy in the subregional integration project, whose exports to its Mercosur partners grew on average 37 percent annually while its exports to the rest of the world grew 11 percent—Mercosur came to be seen as an important market from the standpoint of business.[15]

It was expected that after 1994 the negotiations would move to deepen the integration process. Brazil had implemented its stabilization plan (July 1994), which suggested a greater convergence of the macroeconomic indicators among the Mercosur countries that might attenuate the trade imbalances caused in part by divergent exchange-rate policies. In addition, the international context seemed ripe for continuing increases in the flow of foreign capital into the region.

Integration After 1994

The initiation of the Mercosur customs union coincided with the Mexican financial crisis of late 1994. The lesson of this experience was that the supply of external capital is not unlimited in the presence of mounting current-account deficits; the crisis also made foreign investors question the stability of the emerging markets in Latin America. The response to the crisis varied from country to country, although in general tensions surrounding the integration project rose in the absence of consultations about national adoption of measures that might negatively affect the Mercosur partners. For example, the Brazilian government reduced the time periods for financing textile imports, although the measure in the end was not applied to the Mercosur countries.

In 1995 issues concerning consolidation of stabilization plans dominated the Mercosur countries, with priority given to national solutions, especially for issues that threatened the macroeconomic environment of the member countries. Formal mechanisms for macroeconomic coordination had not been created at that time, which may explain in part such an outcome. Yet that is not the key point. That point is that, initially, the member countries mapped out their national responses independent of a concept of discipline in the integration process—only later did they negotiate the measures, within the framework of the subregional agreement. Brazil's conduct merits special mention, given its preponderant role in the integration scheme.

In December 1995 the commitment to the integration project was reaffirmed through Mercosur's Program of Action to the Year 2000, or Agenda 2000. Implementation of the mechanisms needed to consolidate and improve the customs union has high priority in this program, as do negotiations regarding the deepening of integration as well as external relations and certain other issue areas.[16] Studies concerning greater convergence of tax policies and more substantive negotiations in the area of services are also to be carried out under the action program.

It is beyond the scope of this chapter to describe the status of the negotiations called for in the Program of Action to the Year 2000. It is clear, however, that the program marked the beginning of a new round of negotiations, which were intense in 1996 and 1997. The rule on the application of safeguard clauses regarding imports from third countries was approved; basically, it tracks the rules of the World Trade Organization. Other proposals concerning the environment, consumer defense, and technical rules, among other issues, were addressed and agreement reached. An automotive agreement was signed, providing for free trade within Mercosur as of the year 2000.[17] In December 1997 a normative framework was approved to defend against imports dumped from non-Mercosur countries, along with a protocol on trade in services within Mercosur.

Mercosur's external agenda is one area of Agenda 2000 that has received special emphasis since 1995. In 1993 the Brazilian government proposed the creation of the South American Free Trade Area (SAFTA); the proposal was endorsed by the other members of Mercosur. The proposal, put forth before an automatic tariff reduction program was to take effect in January 1995, aimed at creating a free trade area within ten years encompassing Mercosur, the Andean Pact countries, and Chile. This format for simultaneous negotiations was not implemented, however; instead, priority was accorded to separate agreements between Mercosur and the countries or groups of countries. Agreements were negotiated with Chile (June 1996) and Bolivia (December 1996), and an agreement with the Andean Pact countries is currently being negotiated.[18]

During this period Mercosur also signed two agreements for integration proposals not involving the ALADI countries. On December 15, 1995, an economic cooperation agreement was signed with the European Union. Although that agreement mentions that negotiations on the possible formation of a free trade area will be held, no dates are set, nor has the framework for such negotiations been determined. The agreement strongly emphasizes cooperation with respect to entrepreneurial matters and economic and social reforms.

The second commitment is to the Free Trade Area of the Americas (FTAA), which was proposed by the United States at the Miami Summit in 1994; the goal of the FTAA is the formation of a hemispheric free trade area by 2005. Several working groups were set up, and there have already been three meetings of ministers of trade of the hemisphere;[19] a second hemisphere-wide summit was held in April 1998 in Santiago, Chile, and negotiations to advance the FTAA process are expected to continue.

The United States wanted the negotiations to be carried out by the national states. Nonetheless, the Brazilian proposal, agreed upon by the Mercosur partners, was that the negotiations be held through the already-existing regional groups; this position was ultimately accepted at the Denver meeting of the ministers of trade of the Americas in June–July 1995. In addition, Mercosur has defined a proposal for a three-stage time line for the negotiations, which differs from the U.S. proposal.[20]

Two issues, however, stand out in the post-1995 period. One refers to the format for conducting the integration process. Although total autonomy of national policies in the conduct of macroeconomic matters facilitates quick responses that are well-suited to the particular conditions in each member country, that same autonomy often aggravates situations of conflict. This issue surfaced in 1997, for example, when Brazil, faced with an increase in its trade deficits, implemented measures to reduce the time frame for financing imports; the measures were initially announced as being generally applicable, drawing fire from Brazil's Mercosur partners.[21]

The second issue concerns Mercosur's external agenda, which requires that the member countries present themselves as a clearly cohesive entity, not only in legal terms but also in terms of the integration process.

CHALLENGES CONFRONTING MERCOSUR

The process of forming the common market of Mercosur is clearly distinguishable from that of the European Union. The Treaty of Rome (1957), which instituted Europe's common market, began with proposals for community organs, but these are still absent in Mercosur. Similarly, although the convergence of macroeconomic indicators in Europe in the 1980s is attributed in part to the common discipline imposed by the exchange rate system of 1979, in Mercosur there are no formal mechanisms for macroeconomic coordination.[22]

What factors are usually cited to explain Mercosur's institutional options? The integration process is taking place in a context in which the member countries seek, in varying degrees, to consolidate their plans for stabilization and state reform. From this angle, issues such as harmonization of tax policies, formulation of a common exchange rate policy, and even creation of community organizations are made more difficult.

For example, a worsening of the macroeconomic conditions that can effectively threaten stabilization plans now in place raises questions about the degree of discipline that Mercosur can impose. The largest member country of the customs union—Brazil—has yet to attain sufficiently stable conditions and resources so as to assure the macroeconomic stability of the other member countries. In addition, the relatively small size of the Mercosur market for the Brazilian economy would make it unlikely for Brazil's government to renounce the use of measures that could affect the integration process if it were faced with clear threats to its stabilization plan.[23]

Considering the weight of the Brazilian economy in Mercosur, negotiations on policies that demand the harmonization of macroeconomic instruments would tend to be largely influenced by the pace and format of internal reforms in Brazil, thus making it evident that Mercosur itself is not the frame of reference for the economic reforms. Indeed, the reforms are set forth in the context of restructuring the national economies to enable the implementation of measures consistent with a common market, such as freeing up the markets for services and capital.

Nonetheless, if a deepening of the integration process is sought, common mechanisms for coordinating macroeconomic policy must be created, as must common regulatory entities for administering the rules that govern Mercosur. The basic questions for Mercosur are when such rules should be created and whether the positive or the negative effects of those rules will predominate in the integration process. On the positive side, these rules would introduce an element for discipline into the integration process; the negative effect would be that common structures might constrain desired national actions, placing the very process of integration at risk.

There are no easy answers, especially given that decisionmaking under the subregional agreement requires consensus among countries with extremely unequal economic power. Mercosur's challenge is to create sufficiently flexible entities that enable at least grudging consensus on common principles while not treading too heavily on the relative autonomy of the member countries as the common market is built. In the commercial area, for example, as the customs union approaches full implementation, an inquiry is in order on the appropriate structure and instruments for defending trade interests.

With the creation of community mechanisms, each country renounces part of its autonomy in formulating national policies. In part this renunciation is inherent to the integration process. Because all decisions are made independently of the national governments, however, the risk is high for breakdowns of discipline, which then must be negotiated a posteriori. Regardless, this approach may be the most realistic strategy for Mercosur at this time, even though it engenders many tensions among the members that might have been avoided under a different scenario.

Another challenge facing Mercosur is to come up with a clear definition of the direction of the integration process. Although there is a well-defined time line with respect to the customs union, the same is not true of the common market, a discrepancy that partly explains the current institutional setup. The goal of a common market is held out, but there is no coordinated and detailed structure directing and linking the negotiating groups. The announcement of Agenda 2000 in 1995, when the direction of Mercosur was relatively uncertain, reaffirmed the commitment to implement a common trade policy. There has been no similar announcement regarding the common market. Clearly, however, the direction of the proposed common market will depend largely on the effective interests of Argentina and Brazil, the key players in Mercosur.

A third challenge confronting Mercosur can be posed as a question:

How might Mercosur attain a "more dynamic insertion" into world trade, given the simultaneous worldwide trends of multilateralism and regionalism?

Mercosur's current trade patterns are characterized by multilateralism. In 1996 approximately 23.4 percent of the exports from the Mercosur countries went to the European Union, 28.7 percent to the Latin American Integration Association, 15.8 percent to North America, and 16.8 percent to Asia; exports among the Mercosur countries accounted for 19 percent of total exports (the total does not equal 100 percent because of rounding). The multilateralism of Mercosur's trade is a reflection of the structure of Brazilian exports, which account for 63.6 percent of total exports from the region, and Argentina's, which account for 31.5 percent. The main difference is in the relatively greater weight of the ALADI market for Argentina, and consequently the smaller shares for the European, North American, and Asian markets, as compared with Brazil. The external sales of Paraguay and Uruguay are mostly to other Mercosur countries.

The multilateral character of Brazil's trade and the relatively small size of the Mercosur market suggest the ongoing need for efforts to expand relations with other regions. In addition, strengthening Mercosur as an integrated subregional space demands deepening the economic integration process. If multilateralism is not relegated to second-tier status, Mercosur could provide a special opportunity for the formation of regional undertakings, thus building an integrated infrastructure to bolster the competitiveness of the region's products in world markets, establishing disciplines that consolidate the process of stabilization in the region, and attracting foreign direct investment.

The foreign relations agenda of Mercosur should give priority to entering into agreements in South America. This conclusion flows inevitably from the renegotiation of the historical legacy of ALADI,[24] yet in the framework of free trade agreements, it could also reflect a geopolitical strategy aimed at strengthening Mercosur within the hemisphere and internationally. The agreements already reached with Chile and Bolivia and the negotiations under way with the Andean Pact countries fit into this context. Expanding the network of free trade agreements with South American countries would give Mercosur greater bargaining power in negotiations with the developed countries on integration agreements, especially the FTAA.

Economic considerations are another argument for according priority to South America.[25] The costs of adjustment of the productive sectors in a South America–wide process of liberalization are lower than they would be for hemispheric integration. Expanding the South American market yields economies of scale, which translate into greater efficiency that would, in turn, attenuate the adjustment costs that would very likely result from entering into free trade agreements with the United States or the European Union or both. These propositions are true, however, only if Latin American integration takes place congruent with openness to the rest of the world and with agreements that are not mainly long lists of exceptions to intraregional free trade. Nonetheless, for Mercosur to effectively draw its members and consolidate a South American position in international forums, it must gain visibility through more encompassing commitments to integration. This point was highlighted in the framing of proposals for negotiating the FTAA, given that hemispheric working groups already address a thoroughgoing range of issues.[26]

Finally, Mercosur has before it the opportunity to improve the well-being of the societies in its member countries by contributing to renewed sustainable growth in the region. This challenge should be answered in large measure by the national governments, but the potential that Mercosur possesses for generating economic and social cooperation should not be ignored. In economic terms, gains can be expected from not only special-ization in production and economies of scale but also technical cooperation agreements, joint ventures, and stable rules. In the social area, because inte-gration is a political project, Mercosur can be a vehicle for strengthening democratic societies in the region.[27]

CONCLUSION

It is difficult to imagine a reversal of the integration project set in motion by the Treaty of Asunción. In particular, the concept of subregional integra-tion as a customs union is well consolidated, even though temporary excep-tions to the agreed-upon rules exist.

There is still a long way to go, however, to build the common market. Negotiations have been influenced by the objectives of consolidating stabi-lization plans as well as by the differential pace of internal reforms in each country. In general, Mercosur has not been the frame of reference when changes in economic measures or market regulations have been sought.

Mercosur's agenda for external relations nevertheless suggests the importance of presenting a united front on the various issues addressed in new trade agreements. In particular, the demands of the negotiating process for the FTAA have demonstrated the need to strengthen common positions to give Mercosur credibility in hemispheric relations. Common positions do not require that common measures be implemented, though doing so would further the integration process.

The pace of negotiations has intensified, especially since 1996. As new rules requiring common responses are created, the issue of Mercosur's institutional status increasingly comes to the fore. One aspect of that issue concerns the advisability of inducing the integration process through the creation of supranational mechanisms, as happened in Europe. This question is a sensitive one for Mercosur, whose member countries are still consolidating their national plans for stabilization and state reform. It is especially sensitive for Brazil, whose dynamism in foreign trade is not limited to Mercosur.[28]

The creation of supranational institutions is problematic for Mercosur. On the one hand, the absence of any community entity with either advisory or decisionmaking power gives rise to conflicting responses that must be resolved a posteriori through political decisions, which are not always transparent. Particularly in areas in which negotiations are well advanced—trade policy, for example—some form of community organization needs to be considered. On the other hand, the question is one of creating supranational organizations that will impose discipline and direct the integration process by, for example, defining a common exchange rate policy. The current feasibility of adopting measures of this kind is in doubt.

Insofar as the political economy of regionalism is concerned, the formation of regional agreements might be viewed in three different ways.[29] The first interpretation favors institutional factors conceived from a supranational point of view, in which regional institutions are cooperation mechanisms that reduce uncertainties, lower the costs of public goods, and help governments in the fulfillment of established rules. The second one is critical of the institutionalist approach; it stresses that the formalization (or lack) of regional arrangements depends on the power relationships between the states and on their objectives. The third interpretation bases its explanation of regionalism on domestic interests.

My approach in this chapter was not to analyze the benefits and problems stemming from the creation of a discipline-imposing supranational institution within Mercosur but rather to provide a theoretical base from which to assess the motivations for the creation of such institutions. Accordingly, I favored a realistic approach in which the power relationships and objectives of different states, together with their domestic interests, explain the creation of regional institutions. In this context, given the huge asymmetry in the distribution of economic power among the members of Mercosur, as well as the perception that the domestic political agenda of the group's largest member—Brazil—is not entirely subordinate to the logic of the process of integration, it is highly unlikely that supranational arrangements that are not seen entirely as mechanisms to further domestic interests will be created. Yet because one of the objectives of Mercosur is to strengthen the region's international negotiating position, the perception exists that Mercosur's institutional mechanisms must be deepened to guarantee the group's visibility in the international arena.

The basic issue is not simply whether a supranational institutional framework will lead to discipline for integration. Indeed, it is feasible to accede to a supranational framework only if the participant countries believe such arrangements will help them make the most of their efforts to achieve their domestic policy objectives. On proposing a common market as a goal, the Mercosur countries would appear to be accepting that proposition. Nonetheless, the economies involved in the negotiating process in Mercosur are still, in many areas, defining the institutional and economic reforms they would like to adopt. This observation is especially true for Brazil, the largest economy in the subregional agreement. Seen in this light, not all of the requisites for a broad community institutional framework are present, although nothing stands in the way of seeking some mechanism for community coordination.

NOTES

1. Mercosur is the acronym for Mercado Común del Sur, or Common Market of the South.
2. The emphasis placed on the capital goods sector in PICE was no accident. See Roberto Lavagna, "Integração Argentina-Brasil: Origem, Resultados e Perspectivas," in *Cone Sul: A Economia Política da Integração,* ed. Pedro da Motta Veiga (Rio de Janeiro: Fundação Centro de Estudos do Comércio Exterior, 1991), 27–60.
3. The treaty was approved by the congresses of Brazil and Argentina in August 1989.
4. The Treaty of Asunción originally established ten subgroups: trade, customs, technical standards, trade-related fiscal and monetary policy, overland transportation, maritime transportation, industrial and technology policy, agricultural policy, energy policy, and coordination of macroeconomic policies. A subgroup on labor, employment, and social security was formed later.
5. The number of excepted products was relatively small: Argentina (394), Brazil (324), Paraguay (439), and Uruguay (960), in a universe of at least 10,000 items of merchandise.
6. Rules of origin, in principle, would not be necessary in unified markets that require the adoption of common external tariffs in relation to third countries. The dispute-settlement mechanism was defined as transitory; a definitive instrument was to be implemented after 1994.
7. The working subgroups under the GMC are now communications, mining, technical regulations, financial matters, transportation and infrastructure, industry, agriculture, energy, labor relations, employment, and social security.
8. The technical committees created cover tariffs, nomenclature and classification of goods, customs matters, standards and trade disciplines, policies that distort competition, unfair practices and safeguard clauses, consumer advocacy, nontariff barriers, and the automotive and textile sectors.
9. All of the Mercosur countries maintain national lists of exceptions to the common external tariff, which will lapse on December 31, 2000, for Argentina, Brazil, and Uruguay; Paraguay has a longer time frame, until 2006. The lists allow for the inclusion of no more than 300 products, and 399 for Paraguay.

10. Honorio Kume and Ricardo A. Markwald, "As Perspectivas do Mercosul: Configuração da Estrutura Produtiva e Convergência Macroeconômica," in *Perspectivas da economía brasileira* (Rio de Janeiro: Instituto de Pesquisa Econômica Aplicada, 1994), 205–230.

11. "National treatment" for investment is an expression used in GATT (General Agreement on Tariffs and Trade) and regional agreements, meaning that foreign investment will be treated under the same rules applied to investments by national residents.

12. Miguel Izam, "Evolución, Análisis y Perspectivas del Mercado Común del Sur," working paper LC/R 1706, Economic Commission on Latin America and the Caribbean, Santiago, Chile, 1997.

13. For example, in 1992 the GDP in Argentina grew 8.4 percent; in Brazil, GDP was down 1.1 percent that year.

14. Roberto Bouzas, "La agenda económica del Mercosur: Desafíos de política a corto y mediano plazo," in *Integración y Comercio* (Buenos Aires), 1 (January–April 1996): 64–87.

15. In 1991 Mercosur accounted for 7.3 percent of Brazil's total exports; in 1994 this figure increased to 13.6 percent.

16. These issues are environment, labor relations, employment and social security, culture, health, education, science and technology, police cooperation, and migration.

17. The automotive sector illustrates one of the innumerable points pending in the process of forming a common market. In January 1996 a transition period was agreed upon, respecting the requirements determined by the national governments that link exports and imports, in addition to negotiations to attenuate the trade deficit accumulated by Argentina with Brazil. A process to harmonize incentives in the auto industry also was to be initiated. The same year the Brazilian government implemented special tax incentives for setting up assembly plants in the states of the Brazilian northeast, sparking protests from Argentina.

18. As a customs union Mercosur must observe the same tariff levels with respect to its trading partners. As for ALADI, the member countries negotiated different preferential tariff lists. In this way, given the requirement to harmonize the concessions inherited (the historical legacy), the directive was to engage in wide-ranging trade liberalization. Mexico, given its participation in the North American Free Trade Agreement (NAFTA), requires special negotiations that, to date, have proven difficult.

19. The failure of the U.S. Congress to approve fast-track authority, which is the delegation of power to the president to negotiate trade agreements and submit them to Congress for approval without the possibility of amendment, delayed negotiations for the FTAA.

20. The Mercosur proposal is a three-stage negotiation. The first is to include measures to facilitate trade, and the second is to reach convergence where required to be able to prepare the conditions for the third stage, which would be negotiations for market access. The timetable for hemispheric integration is to begin in 2005. The United States proposes assigning priority to the issue of market access and the possibility of sectoral agreements, as in trade in electronic goods, for example. This guideline is not accepted by Mercosur, whose members support an agreement based on the principle of the "single undertaking," which presumes that agreements are signed only after solutions have been arrived at in all the areas being negotiated.

21. Special conditions were later negotiated for the Mercosur countries.

22. The setting of relatively fixed parities among the European countries may

have contributed to the search for monetary policy goals, and then for indicators of convergent rates of inflation.

23. Examples of such measures include making changes in the lists of exceptions to the common external tariff and the creation of new lists brought on by the stabilization process.

24. The historical legacy refers to the tariff preferences negotiated under ALADI through bilateral agreements.

25. An agreement, in the short term, for full hemispheric liberalization that incorporates the United States would give impetus to the process of unilateral liberalization in the case of an economy such as Brazil's. That decision may be made, but its justification would be related more to changes in national policy directives, thereby preserving the multilateral nature of the liberalization process.

26. Such issues include market access, technical barriers, countervailing duties and antidumping investigations, government procurement, investment, services, and defense of competition.

27. One example: Mercosur adopted a commitment to maintain democratic governments when a political crisis in Paraguay was narrowly averted.

28. The sensitivity of the issue is also partly true for Argentina, although that country has increased its dependence on trade with Brazil. Whereas Argentina accounts for 10.8 percent of Brazilian exports, Brazil accounts for some 28 percent of Argentine exports.

29. Edward D. Mansfield and Helen V. Milner, "The Political Economy of Regionalism: An Overview," in *The Political Economy of Regionalism,* ed. Edward D. Mansfield and Helen V. Milner (New York: Columbia University Press, 1997), 1–19.

2

Brazil in Mercosur: Reciprocal Influence

Pedro da Motta Veiga

In 1995 Brazil accounted for approximately 70 percent of the total gross domestic product (GDP) of Mercosur. So situated, its economic performance, domestic policies, and negotiating position within the bloc have a major impact on the overall development of the integration process, its methodology, and its negotiating agenda.

First, Brazil's economic performance and the design of its macro- and microeconomic policies (especially industrial and foreign trade policies) largely define the other partners' perceptions of the costs and benefits of integration. The emergence of tensions among the member states of Mercosur, as well as their capacity to absorb and manage them, depends heavily on these factors. Second, Brazil's negotiating position is certainly one of the main explanations for Mercosur's current profile, halfway between a free trade area and a customs union with few mechanisms for institutionalization and limited positive discrimination for the benefit of the smaller economies of the bloc.

This relationship between Brazil's negotiating position and the model and dynamics of integration has been more evident since 1994, when the automatic and universal mechanisms of liberalization implemented in 1990 completed their cycle; then a new stage began, one in which new mechanisms should predominate, based on thematic or sectoral negotiations and a logic of exchanging concessions among the member states. Because this change coincided in Brazil with the government's partial review of industrial and foreign trade policy, however, Brazil's influence over the dynamics of Mercosur is a hindrance to addressing the so-called agenda of consolidation and deepening of the customs union.[1]

In this chapter I discuss Brazil's insertion into Mercosur, an integration process in which Brazil unquestionably plays the leading role. With this in mind, the following section describes the elements that shape Brazil's negotiating position in Mercosur, emphasizing the domestic policies geared to industry and foreign trade. The next section covers the traditional explanation for Brazil's negotiating stance, which holds that because the economic gains Brazil derives from Mercosur are necessarily very limited, that country's strategy of moderating its efforts to deepen the subregional integration process is rational. The final section presents conclusions.

BRAZIL'S STRATEGY IN MERCOSUR
AND DOMESTIC ECONOMIC POLICY

Brazil's negotiating position in Mercosur reflects the predominant evaluation among policymakers about the costs and benefits of the integration process. Given the economic and political weight of Brazil in the bloc, this evaluation closely conditions the dynamics of the negotiations as well as the agenda, its priorities, and so on.

The prevalent assessment in Brazil is that the gains from trade liberalization in the subregion are important but that incentives to adopt policy initiatives that might help hurdle a wide array of obstacles to the free circulation of goods and services within the bloc are limited, as are incentives to take the customs union further in the direction of a common market. This evaluation is based on the idea that the asymmetry in size among the national markets of the bloc curtails the potential benefits of Mercosur to Brazil, and so a negotiating agenda in which exchanges of concessions involve regulations considered fundamentally domestic in nature is unjustified.

This idea alone, however, cannot fully explain Brazil's negotiating position in Mercosur. If the small size of the markets of other countries were the most important factor behind Brazil's moderate position in Mercosur, Brazil might be expected to enthusiastically support the formation of the Free Trade Area of the Americas (FTAA), given the potential privileged access to large national markets included in this new proposal. Yet this enthusiasm does not exist, suggesting that market size is of small significance as an explanation for Brazil's negotiating position in integration processes, especially Mercosur.

In general, two factors seem to shape Brazil's defensive position in integration processes as different from each other as are Mercosur and the FTAA: first, the predominance of the interests of the import-competing sectors over the export-oriented sectors in determining industrial policy and foreign trade policy, and second, the hegemony of a strategic vision of foreign policy that is expressed in notions such as "building a regional power" and in concepts such as "autonomy of development," to the detriment of considerations informed by a geoeconomic and commercial perspective. A more careful analysis of the latter factor is beyond the scope of this chapter, although the addition of this variable to the analysis of Brazil's participation in integration processes goes further in explaining Brazil's position than reference to the size of the markets involved, the economic costs and benefits potentially associated with these processes, and so on.

As for the political economy of industrial and foreign trade policy, Araújo recalled that "the basic mechanism for promoting economic integration is the interest of export industries in new market opportunities."[2] If microeconomic policies are attuned to the interests and pressures of the import-competing sectors, however, it would be understandable for Brazil in external negotiations to reflect concerns related to control of the domestic market and maintain considerable room for maneuver in the handling of these policies, independent of the size of its partners.

The weight of the national developmentalist vision on Brazil's negotiating strategy in the FTAA appears to be the most significant explanation for Brazil's negotiating position.[3] In Mercosur, the evolution of microeconomic policies for industry and foreign trade offers the most adequate key to interpreting the positions that Brazil has adopted within the bloc over the past seven years.

Indeed, from 1990 to 1994, trade liberalization was practically the only major industrial policy initiative of the federal government in Brazil, which was a departure from the country's long-standing tradition of activism that combined a wide array of sectoral and regional promotion schemes with widespread protectionism through tariff and nontariff barriers. It is not by chance that the first head-on attack on the national developmentalist paradigm—the unilateral trade liberalization adopted by the Collor government—occurred in the public policy realm during that period. In the same years Mercosur was established and its timetable for trade liberalization implemented. Thus the tradition of sectoral negotiations within the Latin American Integration Association (Asociación Latinoamericana de Integración, or ALADI) was abandoned, as was the initiative to define a permanent structure of subregional, thematic negotiations conducted by technical groups. A good part of the negotiating agenda set for these groups by the Act of Las Leñas of 1992 involved efforts to identify and later eliminate asymmetries among the domestic policies of the various member states.

The second half of 1994 marked an upsurge in Brazil's commitment to the subregional integration process. In fact, in view of the absolute priority accorded to the stabilization policy domestically (the Plano Real), the commitments signed by Brazil in Mercosur were implemented by guaranteeing the supply of the domestic market and maximizing the exposure of local producers to competition from abroad (for instance, the entry into force of the common external tariff was anticipated). It was also around this time that an agreement was reached on the institutional structure of Mercosur (the Protocol of Ouro Preto), an issue that Brazil had always been reticent to negotiate, even when its commitment to Mercosur was at its height.

Beginning in 1995, Brazil's negotiating position in Mercosur changed significantly, directly reflecting a partial reversion of the liberal trend in industrial and foreign trade policy in Brazil. Certain processes embody this change:

- First, policymakers concluded that once the time line for unilateral tariff reductions, the Mercosur transition period, and the multilateral negotiations of the Uruguay Round on the General Agreement on Tariffs and Trade were all concluded, Brazil would have to "digest" this three-way move in the direction of liberalization, removing from its foreign trade agenda any initiatives that might entail additional commitments to open up.
- Second, the Mexican crisis of late 1994 ushered in a process of managing imports, mostly through tariffs, to avoid a major deterioration in the trade balance, which ran a deficit in 1995 after more than a decade of large positive balances. The deterioration in the balance of trade could, in the short term, "contaminate" the stabilization strategy, which is grounded in the nominal rate of exchange. Rates of the common external tariff (CET) moved generally upward, thereby discouraging imports of durable and nondurable consumer goods.
- Third, as the exchange rate appreciated after implementation of the Plano Real, industry came under greater exposure to foreign competition. Less competitive business sectors suffered significant damage, which led to a resurgence of protectionist pressure from industry. Some sectors benefited from the introduction of import quotas (toys and clothes), and the federal government introduced other measures to defend domestic trade (antidumping mechanisms, for example) established in the Uruguay Round.
- Fourth, to deal with the macro- and microeconomic impacts of exchange rate appreciation and with doubts about the sustainability of the stabilization strategy, government policy gradually moved in a new direction regarding industry and exports. New instruments to provide incentives for investment were introduced—the classic (and extreme) example involves the automotive industry—to help sectors undergoing restructuring and to attract producers capable of replacing imports (manufacturers of telecommunications equipment, for example). As for exports, the government expanded its support through public financing (including subsidies), elimination of taxes that had been levied on exports of semimanufactured goods, and export loan guarantees. This trend accelerated in the

second half of 1997 when deterioration of the international business climate and its potential impact on the sustainability of the Plano Real became apparent.

In other words, in contrast to Brazil's liberal industrial and foreign trade policies of earlier years, which included aggressive adoption of strong policy initiatives in Mercosur, today's "neo-activism" in those policy areas calls for Brazil to distance itself, in relative terms, from its subregional commitments and from consolidation of the customs union, even though the Brazilian authorities continue to avow the importance of these agreements.

From the standpoint of the integration process, the problem now is that this cooling of Brazil's negotiating position emerged precisely as the growth in trade flows and investment within Mercosur signaled the economic interdependence of its member states, thus intensifying the demands, especially on the part of Brazil's partners, for the member states to adopt convergent policies. Indeed, given the economic weight of Brazil in Mercosur, the conjunction of that country's unilateral activism with the considerable degree of interdependence within the bloc maximizes the potential that its national policies will distort trade flows, and especially investment flows, to the detriment of the smaller economies.

Interestingly, Brazil has undertaken major regulatory reforms to foster greater liberalization (privatization and deregulation of services, for example), yet there is little echo of these domestic changes in the country's international negotiations, even in Mercosur. As reported in one recent study, "The very evolution of Brazil's domestic regulations in areas such as services, government procurement, investment, intellectual property rights, and competition policy leaves Brazil in a comfortable position for negotiating these issues" in bilateral or multilateral forums.[4] More important, "One can judge that the country, interested in attracting external investment in services and industry, benefits from observing the supranational disciplines in areas still considered sensitive in Brazil."[5] Nevertheless, in the external agenda for integration—which in Brazil so faithfully translates into commitment to the national-developmentalist paradigm and the political economy of the industrial and foreign trade policies—there appears to be resistance to translating these emerging domestic trends into initiatives to deepen the "Mercosur preference."

THE IMPORTANCE OF MERCOSUR FOR BRAZIL: A REASSESSMENT

From the outset of the integration process, the political will of the national governments was a key variable in explaining the dynamism of Mercosur. Starting from a low level of economic interdependence, integration at first came to depend on a political dynamic, but with the impressive increase in trade flows among the Mercosur countries from 1990 to 1993, economic interests were consolidated and the process became less directly dependent on the political will of the governments.

The skepticism prevalent in academic and business circles with respect to the integration process was overcome. Intergovernmental negotiations proved to be an important learning and confidence-building process for the national bureaucracies, but the idea remains that furthering the integration process would entail more costs than benefits for Brazil in terms of loss of autonomy in domestic policymaking. When an institutional component is added to the proposal to further integration, rejection is even greater in Brazil, because institutions are seen as the formal confirmation of that loss of autonomy.

Mercosur accounts for only 15 percent of Brazilian exports, but the importance for Brazil of the integration process now under way is far greater than one might infer from this figure. At the political-institutional level, the importance of Mercosur is clearer when regionalization is under-stood to allow two simultaneous phenomena: Not only can Brazil engage continuously in negotiations on all the issues that make up the new interna-tional trade agenda but also Mercosur can maximize the political weight of each of its members in all external negotiations, whether conducted indi-vidually or en bloc.

It is more difficult to make the argument that the potential benefits of the integration process for Brazil are greater than current information on trade would suggest, but certain data and information do support that con-clusion:

- Mercosur is responsible for the most important change of the 1990s in the pattern of Brazil's foreign trade, especially its exports. In 1990 Mercosur accounted for 4.2 percent of Brazilian exports and for 11.2 percent of its imports; by 1996 these figures had climbed to 15.5 and 15.6 percent, respectively. From 1990 to 1996, Brazil's exports to other Mercosur countries grew 33.3 percent a year, whereas for the rest of the world such growth was only 5.0 percent; in 1996 exports to Mercosur grew 20.6 percent, although exports to the rest of the world declined slightly (–0.1 percent).
- Mercosur's influence on Brazil's export performance in the 1990s affects Brazil's foreign sales in several ways: The geoeconomic regions with the greatest growth in exports from 1990 to 1996 are those that share borders with Mercosur countries, and in recent years small and medium-size enterprises have become involved in export activities, largely linked to trade with Mercosur. In addition, the changes observed in the sectoral composition of the pattern of

exports in the 1990s appear to be associated with the expansion of sales by certain industries to Mercosur (machines, auto parts, and chemical products, among others).

- Exports to the countries of Mercosur (and ALADI) performed an important countercyclical function in sectors affected by the considerable growth of imports in the domestic market, as in the case of machinery and machine equipment. These sectors saw their export and import coefficients rise simultaneously throughout the decade (imports much more than exports). Mercosur certainly has something to do with the rise in exports, compensating those sectors for the upsurge in imports.

- Brazil's exports to Argentina (and Mercosur generally) show a pattern qualitatively superior to that observed for exports to the rest of the world, when analyzed in light of criteria such as the degree of technological intensity and the factor component of exports, among others.[6] Bosco Machado and Markwald noted that "the institution of Mercosur and the advances of the regional integration process appear to have contributed decisively to deepening this differentiation."[7] It is important to note that exports with high technological content have important, positive spillover effects in the economy, such as better worker skills, adoption of quality standards, and so on.

- Brazil's foreign investments in Mercosur grew significantly, climbing from U.S.$180 million in 1991 to U.S.$350 million in 1995, with that growth distributed among several segments of industry (auto parts, metallurgy, food and beverages, and chemicals, among others) and services (financial and health services and advertising, for example). In other words, some studies suggest that Mercosur might be playing an important role in the internationalization of Brazilian firms and groups, thereby helping diminish one of these companies' main competitive deficits—namely, their limited involvement in international activities other than exporting.

Considering these facts, it would appear that the economic importance of Mercosur to Brazil could be much greater than is generally believed to be the case.

This argument is buttressed by the finding that there is still a vast array of fiscal and regulatory barriers to the free circulation of goods, services, and investments among the member states of Mercosur, and thus the potential of the expanded market is far from being fully exploited. Eliminating those barriers that perpetuate the fragmentation of the expanded market and deepening integration can certainly create new business opportunities that Brazilian firms could seize, given the preferences they already enjoy and the ones they will receive as well as their geographic proximity to and knowledge of the market.

The potential for convergence of Brazilian business interests with the effort to consolidate and deepen the customs union clearly exists, though meeting that potential would mean renouncing certain instruments that may appear to benefit Brazilian industry but in reality distort trade and investment flows and are especially prejudicial to the smaller economies of the subregion.

Curiously, more than a reassessment of Mercosur's economic importance to Brazil, the pressure to negotiate the FTAA could lead that country to adopt a position less resistant to issues that so far have been considered to have low priority. In fact, Brazil's proposal to make subregional integration schemes the building blocks of the FTAA requires that Mercosur take up the issues and subjects pertaining to the agenda for deepening the customs union.

SUMMARY

In this chapter I have evaluated Brazil's participation in Mercosur by analyzing some of the factors—particularly industrial policy and foreign trade—that influenced the evolution of Brazil's negotiating position in the integration process. In this context, the political daring Brazil displayed in Mercosur from 1990 to 1994 is the counterpoint to the adoption of domestic policies very much marked by liberalization. That period may itself be considered a temporary hiatus within the Brazilian tradition of active industrial and export policies, a tradition that has found expression once again under the Cardoso administration.

I also reexamined the notion that the gains Brazil is making and can expect to obtain with Mercosur are limited, which, if true, would legitimate the country's relative indifference about consolidating and deepening the customs union. As it turns out, however, there are solid indications that Mercosur's importance in both political-institutional and economic terms goes well beyond what is suggested by general data on Brazil's trade flows with its partners. Furthermore, initiatives to consolidate and deepen Mercosur particularly interest Brazilian exporters and companies that invest abroad, which are especially well positioned to capture a large part of the new business that Mercosur might generate.

NOTES

1. Inter-American Development Bank/Institute for the Integration of Latin America and the Caribbean, *Informe Mercosur* 2 (January–June 1997).

2. J. Tavares Araújo, Jr., "Desempenho exportador e integração econômica no hemisfério ocidental," *Revista Brasileira de Comércio Exterior* 51 (April–June 1997) (Rio de Janeiro, Fundação Centro de Estudos do Comércio Exterior): 51–59.

3. E. Vargas Garcia, "O pensamento dos militares em política internacional," *Revista Brasileira de Política Internacional* 40, no. 1 (January–June 1997): 18–40.

4. Pedro da Motta Veiga and João Bosco Machado, "A ALCA e a estratégia negociadora brasileira," *Revista Brasileira de Comércio Exterior* 51 (April–June 1997) (Rio de Janeiro, Fundação Centro de Estudos do Comércio Exterior): 33–42.

5. Ibid.

6. João Bosco Machado and Ricardo Markwald, "Dinâmica recente do processo de integração do Mercosul," discussion paper 128, Fundação Centro de Estudos do Comércio Exterior (Rio de Janeiro), 1997.

7. Ibid.

3

Mercosur's Complex Political Agenda

Monica Hirst

Friends were quite hard to find, old authors say,
But now they stand in everybody's way.
                    —*William Blake,* Miscellaneous Epigrams

Economic integration has become Mercosur's driving motivation during the past several years, thanks to the extraordinary expansion of intraregional trade and cross-border investment. Nonetheless, it would be an error to characterize Mercosur as an integration effort that involves only economic interaction. Other chapters of this book exhaustively explore the nature and prospects of the economic integration project; this one addresses the noneconomic developments of Mercosur, focusing particularly on the relationship between Argentina and Brazil, which is at the core of the regional integration success story in the Southern Cone.

Although it is useful to trace Mercosur's origins back to the mid-1980s, it is especially important to track the close connection between trade negotiations and domestic and foreign politics since then. Economic integration, convergent foreign policy goals, and security cooperation were intertwined in the Southern Cone before Mercosur came to life, yet that parallelism does not constitute a smooth three-track process. The pace of cooperation in each sphere has varied according to internal political circumstances and transformations in world politics.

RELATIONSHIPS AMONG COUNTRIES
OF THE SOUTHERN CONE BEFORE MERCOSUR

As Argentina, Brazil, and Uruguay underwent the transition to democracy, active presidential diplomacy led to unprecedented coordination of foreign policy. Regional integration was then sought as a political tool to consolidate broader goals aimed at reversing the dark ages of authoritarianism, intraregional antagonism, economic crisis, and international marginalization. The foreign ministries of Argentina and Brazil began to develop a cooperative agenda on various issues, including world politics, economic integration, and technological cooperation. In 1986 the presidents of those countries set forth the Program for Integration and Cooperation, a formal mechanism to stimulate closer ties.

Of course, the transition to democracy was considerably different in each country, especially in the areas of civil-military relations and past violations of human rights. These differences, however, did not curtail cooperation on intraregional political and security matters. Though the military played only a marginal role in the redesign of foreign policy in these countries, their presence was still crucial in all matters dealing with defense.

Macroeconomic instability was an obstacle to reaching integration goals for trade and investment, but the final escalation of the Cold War brought more convergence of foreign policy. Argentina and Brazil took common stances on various foreign affairs issues, including the crisis in Central America, the Uruguay Round of negotiations on the General Agreement on Tariffs and Trade, nuclear nonproliferation regimes, and the South Atlantic peace zone. The most important step in interstate security relations was toward nuclear cooperation: The gradual enforcement of confidence-building measures deactivated earlier fears of a nuclear arms race between Argentina and Brazil, both of which were reluctant to adhere to international nonproliferation regimes and chose to coordinate that stance. As for economic relations, regional integration initiatives had produced only poor results, and the countries shared concerns about high inflation. Both countries faced a governance crisis serious enough to jeopardize the continuity of democratic transition.

In short, there were many economic and political commonalities during the first phase of democratization in the countries of Mercosur, particularly between Argentina and Brazil. It became easier to achieve foreign policy coordination than to meet targets for economic integration: The Cold War made it sensible to adopt common defensive postures in international affairs, and the lack of economic stability circumscribed interstate trade and undermined efforts to consolidate a regional integration scheme. Nevertheless, political elites at least agreed on the importance of regionalism. Contacts among politicians, national bureaucrats, businesspeople, and intellectuals stepped up, and by 1989 conditions were ripe for approval of the Treaty on Integration, Cooperation, and Development between Argentina and Brazil. The treaty, which would transform previous associative efforts into a long-term intergovernmental commitment, was conceived as the first major step toward the creation of a common market open to all countries in South America.

THE REORIENTATION OF FOREIGN
AND ECONOMIC POLICIES IN ARGENTINA AND BRAZIL

A new scenario began to take shape in the late 1980s. New governments came to power in Argentina and Brazil in 1989 and 1990, respectively, and with them came a gradual reorientation of foreign and domestic economic policies. Although both countries had approached world politics similarly at the outset of this period, internal political developments eventually caused their outlooks to diverge. Over the course of the transformations that had taken place by the end of the Cold War, Argentina and Brazil came to view the pros and cons of the new world order in different ways. The new Argentine government moved toward a special relationship with the United States, which was perceived as the best strategic option for obtaining international credibility and internal political stability. Brazil, though, after overcoming domestic turmoil in the 1990–1992 period, preserved a foreign policy stance that valued autonomy in world affairs, resisting U.S. attempts to expand leadership prerogatives in the inter-American realm. Meanwhile, the Brazilian foreign ministry set as its first priority an agenda based on trade agreements and cooperative initiatives with its South American neighbors.

The differing positions of the Argentine and Brazilian governments are illustrated by their contrasting perceptions of the nuclear agreement they signed in November 1990. For Brazilian military and diplomatic circles, the mutual acceptance of a full-scope nuclear safeguard system, negotiated over the course of five years, symbolized the finish line: It met the pressures of the nuclear powers for a nonproliferation commitment, it would also bestow some prestige in the international community, and it could open the way to other confidence-building measures in Latin America. Argentine officials, however, perceived this agreement as a starting point for updating sensitive technology policies.[1]

With the arrival of economic stability during the last part of Itamar Franco's administration (1992–1994), a new chapter opened in Brazil's foreign affairs. As the country gained credibility internationally, Brazil's perceptions about the changing world order underwent fine-tuning: Relations with Washington gradually became less ticklish, the idea that Brazil had a role to play as "consensus builder" in the international community grew, and defensive attitudes gave way to "participative" diplomacy in world affairs. Whereas in Argentina the redefinition of foreign policy touched both the diplomatic and defense spheres, Brazil reviewed its stands on world politics more easily than it did those on international security matters. The progressive dismantling of military control over defense policies led to a gradual process of adherence to international nonproliferation regimes, however, and to the acceptance of nonmilitary domestic control of sensitive technology.

Although Argentina and Brazil's foreign policy convergences decreased, common economic interests grew between the two countries. The negotiation of the Treaty of Asunción (1991) and the fast response of the economies to the new rules of the game in intraregional trade generated unprecedented investment and commercial cross-border flows. The political motivations behind these results had more to do with the effects of economic stability, open trade policies, and democratic continuity than with common foreign policy goals. The idea that stable economies and long-lasting democracies would increase international credibility replaced the belief that common political grounds in world affairs would expand mutual political leverage.

Commonalties in world politics were no longer a given. For Argentina, it was crucial to coordinate economic integration with regional cooperative security. Though conceived as parallel alternatives, participation in Mercosur and full alignment with the United States were to evolve in the same direction; a cooperative security scheme and creation of the Free Trade Area of the Americas (FTAA) would become complementary processes. Brazil's expectations were quite different: The Asunción treaty was perceived as a first step toward creation of a free trade area throughout South America, cooperative security schemes were to be avoided, confidence-building measures should be stimulated, and the extension of the North American Free Trade Agreement (NAFTA) to South America could not overshadow Mercosur.

REACHING CONSENSUS ON REGIONAL INTEGRATION

Interstate relations among Mercosur members entered a new phase in the mid-1990s as the associative process expanded and strengthened. Intraregional interaction generated for the first time genuine dynamics of interdependence between the economies of the area. More and more, regional integration rested upon a new set of connections between domestic and international interests, linked by a variety of private networks. As in other parts of the world where regionalism had expanded, relations among Argentina, Brazil, Paraguay, and Uruguay were motivated more by economic interests than by common foreign policy goals.[2]

Although differences in foreign policy and international security still existed, Argentina and Brazil tended to downplay their conflictive nature. The growing consensus among political and economic elites on the importance of regional integration helped move the focus of diplomacy from political cooperation to economic integration. Widening and deepening the Mercosur process introduced myriad new items to intergovernmental negotiations, and a growing number of social and economic actors became involved in regional integration. Very rapidly Mercosur faced a challenging external agenda in which integration diplomacy was practiced simultaneously with the European Community (EC), other Latin American trade blocs, the World Trade Organization, and the U.S.-led NAFTA. Close political coordination between Argentina and Brazil became a crucial political condition for successful negotiations. In this context, the U.S. government decision announced at the Miami Summit in late 1994 to guide the creation of a Free Trade Area of the Americas became a political incentive for both countries to consolidate Mercosur. Simultaneous negotiations with the European Community were thought to be a way to increase political leverage vis-à-vis the United States.

Mercosur did not advance solely on account of the spillover effects of societal and economic cross-border interactions, however. The Mexican peso crisis at the end of 1994 also was a major catalyst for the Southern Cone integration process. The growing consciousness of political leaders in Argentina and Brazil that their own countries too were vulnerable to erratic global financial movements stimulated an unprecedented sense of mutualism. Indeed, world political-economy events led all of the Mercosur member states to begin thinking in terms of mutualism and thus ushered in a new stage of interstate relationships.

The advance of mutualism among Southern Cone states is one of many examples of the recent worldwide trend toward intergovernmental cooperation based on the identification of common interests and values. As the "subjective similarity" felt by Argentina and Brazil grew after the economic crisis in Mexico, interstate relations expanded.[3] And because Argentine-Brazilian relations were at the core of Mercosur dynamics, bilateral mutualism became a permanent requisite for the deepening and widening of regional integration. Loyalties arose out of convergent perceptions about the need to associate democratic consolidation with economic stability and became the main source of Mercosur's political identity, whereas expansion of worldwide trade and investments in the area became regional integration's main strategic purpose. Thus negotiations with other regional blocs, especially with the EC and NAFTA, were seen as a way to lock in and maximize the shared results of economic reform.

Mercosur politics after early 1995 paid less heed to the political engineering needed for those tasks produced by interdependence than to events transpiring in the international economy, particularly those that engendered financial and monetary global turmoil. Although discussions intensified among and within the member states about the pros and cons of institution-alizing intergovernmental bargaining and intraregional interactions, no major initiative was carried forward to give Mercosur a permanent institu-tional framework. Rather, loose regulations and shallow institutionalism have been maintained at a relatively low political cost. As in other integra-tion projects, regional institution-building initiatives have not accompanied successful economic integration.[4]

The danger that shortfalls in external financing pose for overexposed economies has also influenced Mercosur's external agenda. Although Mexico had been thrown a financial lifeline by the United States in view of their previous trade negotiations, Argentina and Brazil did not expect the same treatment simply because there was a possibility that an FTAA would include Mercosur. Strengthening the Mercosur process in South America was judged to be more useful than sitting in a waiting room while the United States disentangled the domestic legislative restrictions that pre-vented it from moving ahead in hemispheric trade negotiations. Whereas U.S. congressional approval of any post-NAFTA trade agreements had been put in jeopardy by the Mexican crisis, Mercosur initiated negotiations with Bolivia, Venezuela, and Chile (Chile has had a special relationship with Mercosur ever since the signing of the Asunción treaty).

Subjective similarity is grounded not only in shared perceptions of the impact of external economic turmoil but also in the political likeness of Mercosur governments. A growing connection between the prospects for economic integration and the domestic political processes of member states became a prime aspect of expanded regionalism in the Southern Cone. All administrations in the Mercosur area, including that of Chile, can be called center oriented. Whether center-left, center-right, or dead-center, Argentina, Brazil, Uruguay, Paraguay, and Chile have deepened their democratization along similar ideological lines.

Coincidentally, for all these countries regional integration has become a point of consensus among political elites. Although the foreign ministries conduct intergovernmental negotiations, the presidents themselves have assumed a decisive role in the political marketing of Mercosur at home and abroad. Moreover, an association between reelection to government and continuity of Mercosur began to be made in consequence of the recurrent identification of presidents with stable and open economies. Thus, the posi-tive correlation between economic reform, democratization, and regional integration became the essence of Mercosur politics.

Although likemindedness and geographic advantages have counterbal-anced Mercosur's weak institutional framework, they have not eliminated differences in expectations and interests within and among the many societal and economic sectors involved in the expansion of regionalism. The politicization of costs and benefits of shallow institutionalism have become part of everyday life within Mercosur political circles.

DIFFERING PERCEPTIONS IN
ARGENTINA AND BRAZIL ON FOREIGN POLICY

Argentina and Brazil's political interest in strengthening Mercosur did not soften their foreign policy differences. Subtle encapsulation was the solution found by their foreign ministries, as they were both concerned with the impact of negative politicization on the regional integration project. Many sore points were resolved automatically as the Brazilian government reviewed its positions on international security and foreign policy matters. For example, Brazil adhered to the nonproliferation treaty and the Missile Technology Control Regime, enforced domestic legislation controlling sensitive technology exports, and became an active participant in peacekeeping operations of the United Nations (UN). For such international issues as the environment, drug trafficking, and human rights, Brazil replaced its formerly defensive attitudes with positive diplomacy in multilateral forums.

Although these initiatives certainly helped defuse tensions with the United States, the Brazilian foreign ministry did not see them as a revival of old-style alignment with Washington. Hence, their perceptions did not converge with those of Argentine officials, who fully supported U.S. hemispheric security proposals. On several occasions Argentina has been conspicuous among its neighbors and partners for its pro-U.S. orientation in world politics and security matters.[5] In defense ministerial meetings held in Williamsburg (1995) and Bariloche (1997), these differences hindered efforts to move forward on procedures for hemispheric cooperative security.

Such discrepancies in world politics, though not ignored, were played down and suspended from public diplomacy as bilateral economic ties deepened. Moreover, important initiatives were set out to strengthen the political dimension of Mercosur. Two decisions came at the 1996 San Luis presidential summit: First, a democratic clause was added to the Mercosur process, whereby member states agreed to sanction governments that failed to maintain a democratic order; second, a mechanism was agreed upon for political coordination between Argentina and Brazil. The following year Argentina and Brazil signed the Rio Declaration, which defined the status reached by bilateral relations as a "strategic alliance." At that stage, adding a democratic clause to Mercosur had double significance: It strengthened the political grounds of regional integration, and it sent a clear message to Paraguay, for which the pro-democratic coordination between Argentina and Brazil had been a crucial externality for its own continuity of democracy since 1993.

Nonconvergent foreign policies did not fit easily into the new strategic partnership between Argentina and Brazil—the transformation of external expectations into concrete, long-term political options challenged mutual political tolerance. While Argentina concluded negotiations with the United States as an extra–North Atlantic Treaty Organization (NATO) ally, Brazil moved ahead with its candidacy for a permanent seat on the United Nations Security Council (UNSC). The lack of reciprocal support for these initiatives was made public in both countries in 1997. Argentine officials opposed Brazil's candidacy, suggesting instead that a permanent Latin American seat on the UNSC should rotate among the countries of the region. Meanwhile, Brazilian diplomatic circles considered the accord between Argentina and the United States to be an unnecessary, unwanted stimulus for a U.S. military presence in South America. These controversies did not have a salutary effect on Argentine-Brazilian relations.

Public perceptions of the significance of foreign policy discrepancies have not been identical on both sides. Brazilian political society seems to believe that Washington intends to weaken any Southern Cone coalition in world affairs, and it associates Argentina's pro-U.S. policies with that belief. A corollary belief is that the Argentina–Brazil–United States triangle is a crucial political variable for balancing power distribution in the Americas. In other words, Brazilian concerns are geared less to Argentina than to the United States, which is perceived as a major constraint on Brazil's pursuit of its national interest.

Although Argentine political society consensually adheres to the idea of a long-standing relationship with its biggest Mercosur partner, it has not completely purged its unease of earlier years about Brazil's mounting relative power. Indeed, Argentines center their apprehensions on the expansion of Brazilian power, with beliefs about relations with Brazil falling into two camps. One side holds that the expansion of Brazil's presence in world politics and economics is not a zero-sum game so long as common interests are preserved. Moreover, those in this camp think that Brazil might share its expanded power with Argentina in exchange for the support and confidence offered by its southern neighbor. In this scenario, a permanent UN seat for Brazil would be a potential asset for Mercosur, and full alignment with the United States would not be regarded as a safe strategic option. The other side, however, endorses the idea that political alignment with the United States must be maintained to counterbalance the expansion of economic ties with the Brazilian economy. Although reckoned as an extraordinary accomplishment, the fact that 30 percent of Argentina's exported goods go to Brazil is also a reason for concern about the possibility of becoming too dependent on Brazil. According to this perception a two-track strategy is a source of equilibrium for Argentina in foreign affairs. In either case, the United States is not perceived as a menacing actor vis-à-vis national interests, and relations with Brazil are increasingly accepted as a shaping factor in domestic and external matters.

Though foreign policy differences have been maintained, officials in Argentina and Brazil have gradually shunted politicization aside. It became important for both governments to transmit the idea that recent initiatives in world affairs would be faced as legitimate options of post–Cold War politics. For Brazil, adjustment to the new international order implied the need to participate in the ongoing process of change in the distribution of power among states. It also led to a realistic assumption regarding the growth of its own leverage in world affairs, one that justified its "upward mobility." Thus permanent membership in the UN Security Council became an important flag in Brazilian foreign policy, even though support from Latin American countries was harder to come by than extraregional encouragement. Argentina, for its part, thought its extra-NATO alliance with the United States to be a step that would lock in the changes made in recent years in domestic civil-military relations and in international defense policies.

Although it is true that, because of power asymmetries, foreign policy differences are less relevant to Brazil than to Argentina, both countries have no choice but to cope with the consequences of each other's unilateral initiatives. U.S.-Argentine military cooperation has expanded notoriously, whereas Brazil has gained new heavyweight supporters for its UNSC candidacy.

Meanwhile, however, divergent foreign policy goals have not impeded the expansion of interstate relations in myriad other spheres. Argentina is now Brazil's largest oil supplier, and after several decades of thoroughgoing reluctance, Petrobras (Brazil's state-owned petroleum company) has agreed to use Argentine gas as a source of energy for the southern part of Brazil. Cross-border connections are being built for mutual consumption of surplus hydroelectricity, and communication facilities are expanding between both countries. Regional infrastructure initiatives, cooperative agendas in education and culture, and heightened interaction among political actors of member states have widened the scope and deepened the level of intra-Mercosur relations. Moreover, aside from these initiatives at the local and federal levels, cross-border interaction has been intense among business sectors, social organizations, and political elites, and interprovincial networking is taking place between the southern states of Brazil and the northern provinces of Argentina.

A new set of military interstate initiatives also has grown out of political commonalties, together with previous cooperative arrangements among member states. Though it is difficult to bridge the gap from economic integration to security cooperation, Mercosur's members have made some progress. As a spontaneous outcome of regional integration, confidence-building measures involving the land, naval, and air military forces of Argentina, Brazil, and Uruguay have been taken. These initiatives have nothing to do with Argentina's idea (supported by the United States) in the early 1990s of forming a cooperative security system in the Americas. In fact, the differences that emerged between Argentina and other Latin American countries, including Brazil, and obstructed that project partially explain why Argentina opted for a solitary security deal with the United States.

The aim of current military cooperation among Mercosur member states, especially Argentina and Brazil, is not an institutionalized defense mechanism or a pluralistic security community. Nevertheless, recent cooperative programs that sprang from the regional integration process have increased confidence and transparency among the militaries of Mercosur countries. From a conceptual standpoint, military doctrines have become less antagonistic to the idea of a no-war zone in the Southern Cone, and conflictive postures have been abandoned in light of both the shared acknowledgment that internal and external threats in the Southern Cone are minimal or nonexistent and the commitment of defense policies in the region to the maintenance of democratic orders. New security approaches are debated annually in strategy symposiums conducted by the senior military staffs of Argentina and Brazil. And although the Mercosur governments have generally shunned institutional solutions, a small-scale operational scheme called Permanent Commission for Coordination was created in April 1997 to address mutual defense matters.

Interaction among Mercosur armed forces has taken place at both regional and global levels. Shared participation in UN peacekeeping operations is frequent, as are joint military operations in the border zone. Naval exercises, aimed at better defense of the South Atlantic area, have expanded, and the Argentine and Brazilian air forces have stepped up their cooperation to allow common control of air space as well as development of spatial technology programs.

CONCLUSIONS

The political complexities of Mercosur can be shaped to fit many of the current theoretical debates on international relations. For example, can the nation-state survive in a world dominated by a global agenda? Where will the world's tendency toward expansion of regionalism lead? No doubt many other questions discussed in the literature on post–Cold War transformations could be posed for Mercosur. But to place Mercosur politics in an analytical framework, I conclude by briefly exploring two particularly useful approaches to understanding transformations occurring after the Cold War.

A helpful, general approach was first employed by John Lewis Gaddis in describing post–Cold War transformations. The forces of integration and forces of fragmentation overlap in various spheres of interstate and intersocietal relations, "producing integrative and disintegrative consequences" at the same time.[6] Hence they should not be interpreted as mutually exclusive alternatives, although their simultaneity can produce tension in regional politics. The difficult coexistence between national sovereignty and a consolidated, interdependent world in fact creates equilibrium, with one force balancing the other.[7]

It is not difficult to identify fragmentary and integrative forces in Mercosur politics. Even though intraregional trade, investment, and the whole set of spillover effects from integration have been beneficial, intra-Mercosur tensions persist in the economic and political spheres. Besides the economic regulatory and juridical-institutional deficits addressed in other chapters of this book, there are political handicaps that could jeopardize the interstate association. Nonconvergent foreign policy goals have diminished Argentina and Brazil's common interests in world politics. Moreover, given a context of fragile institutions, regional integration could become more vulnerable to the negative politicization of international affairs, although presidential diplomacy has heretofore prevented that outcome. On the other hand, common political concerns—namely, the continuity of democratic order and economic stability—have spurred mutual interests in world economics and regional integration. Political commonalties, in turn, are a by-product of subjective similarities and shared challenges in the international economy.

Robert Keohane and Stanley Hoffman, who study decisionmaking and institutional change in the European Community, have suggested that the mix of various factors—among them subjective similarities, the international political economy, and spillover effects, as well as their particular evolution—accounts for member states' politics. Their analysis lent a liberal-democratic interpretation to classical realism as they pondered the most likely political direction of the EC. They give special attention to Germany when they argue: "Can the Community's existence and policies help dampen a rising hegemon's national aspirations so that they remain acceptable to the less powerful states, without at the same time appearing too burdensome to the hegemon?"[8]

Matching regional politics and power asymmetry is indeed a dilemma for advanced economic integration projects. Although the complexities of European political evolution can hardly be compared with Mercosur politics, some points of analogy do exist. Brazil's economic weight in the Southern Cone is similar to Germany's in the European scenario. In addition, Brazil's major partner in the region does not acquiesce easily to Brazilian aspirations in foreign affairs. Nevertheless, strong political and economic commonalties have neutralized such anomalies as well as stimulated new spheres of understanding in political and security matters.

It is also important to mention that the bridges connecting the economic, political, and defense realms and promoting cooperation are not exclusive to Mercosur in the Americas. Dialogue between Mexico and the United States has reached an unprecedented level in recent years, leading to the negotiation in 1996 of an agreement for security cooperation. Similar developments can be observed in Central America. Whereas basic political commitments to peace and democracy were the starting point for reviving previous associative ventures in the area, the upsurge of confidence-building measures can be largely attributed to the expansion of intraregional mutualism that grew out of the Central American System for Integration .

If the Free Trade Area of the Americas becomes a reality, expectations for its results would be similar to those for other free trade projects. Despite those benefits, however, the Mercosur member states—especially those that are reluctant to enter into hemispheric cooperative security agreements—would face new dilemmas. In particular, power asymmetries among the members of the FTAA could turn out to be even more fragmentary than has been the case in Mercosur politics.

NOTES

1. The most important initiatives resulting from the greater cooperation in interstate security affairs were the dismantling of the Condor 2 ballistic missile project, the signature and ratification of the nuclear nonproliferation treaty, and the adherence to the Missile Technology Control Regime.

2. See Miles Kahler, "Regionalism and Institutions: A Comparative Perspective," paper presented at a meeting of the Instituto del Servicio Exterior de la Nación, Buenos Aires, November 1996.

3. See Robert Keohane and Stanley Hoffman, "Institutional Change in Europe in the 1980s," in *The New European Community,* ed. Robert Keohane and Stanley Hoffman (Boulder, Colo.: Westview Press, 1991), p. 24. Keohane and Hoffman use the concept of *subjective similarity* to analyze the political conditions leading to the Single European Act.

4. Kahler, "Regionalism and Institutions."

5. For example, the Argentine government supported the U.S.-UN military intervention in Haiti, and the Menem administration repeatedly voiced anti-Castro

positions. Also, Argentina has been the most important U.S. ally in defense ministry conferences held since 1993.

6. John Lewis Gaddis, "Toward the Post–Cold War," *Foreign Affairs* 70, no. 2 (Spring 1991), p. 109.

7. Ibid., p. 114.

8. Keohane and Hoffman, "Institutional Change," p. 32.

4

Broadening and Deepening: Striking the Right Balance

Félix Peña

Neither in the geographic extension of the territory covered by its preferences and its collective policy disciplines, nor in the depths of those preferences and disciplines, is Mercosur a finished product. To the contrary, it is a
process constantly exposed to forces pressing for the broadening of its geographic area and a deepening of its commitments.

Broadening is understood in terms of the number of countries included
under Mercosur preferences, whether as full or associate members.
Deepening concerns the scope of the commitments undertaken, especially
those that entail preferential economic treatment and the development of
collective policy disciplines.

Both forces, at times, generate conflicting demands. Broadening could
mean a loss of depth in the commitments undertaken and, under extreme
circumstances, could dilute arrangements for preferential treatment. In such
a case, investors and other economic actors would have little incentive to
seek the advantages of the broadened market by operating out of a member
country instead of an associate member country or even a third country.
The message would be that membership in Mercosur makes no difference,
at least in terms of benefiting from the opportunities offered by a broader
market. Deepening, for its part, could complicate the extension of the
advantages of free trade to those Latin American countries not in a position
to undertake commitments similar to those of Mercosur, given the marginal
nature of their trade with the member countries. The message then would
be that of an exclusive and exclusionary club.

Where is the point of balance between broadening and deepening in
any particular moment in a process of integration such as that of Mercosur?
What is the balance that at any given moment can satisfy the interests of
each of its members? These questions cannot be answered in the abstract.
They can only be answered in specific cases and for specific moments.

These are significant questions not only for Mercosur but also for any voluntary economic integration process among sovereign nations—that is, those processes in which states participate because they understand that it is in their national interest, and they do so to the extent that working together continues to be in their interest. These are processes whose vitality and expansion depend heavily upon the perception of each member that it gains more as a participant than as an outsider. The perception of mutual benefits, based upon a dynamic reciprocity of interests, is what keeps the bond of membership strong; achieving this over time is the essence of the methodologies of voluntary economic integration among sovereign nations. Such methodologies consist essentially of policies, formal (and often informal) rules of the game, and institutions that permit the logic of integration (symbolized in Europe by Maastricht) to predominate over the logic of fragmentation (symbolized in Europe by Sarajevo).

Those joining in these types of processes are nations with common interests and objectives. They are like-minded. Their relative situations and motivations may be compatible but not necessarily the same. The differences in the size of their markets and their relative power are disparities that could affect the extent as well as the depth of their alliance.

Therefore, achieving a dynamic equilibrium between broadening and deepening may be fundamental for maintaining the framework of mutual benefit that holds together the bond of association. Given the disparity of situations and motivations, a pronounced imbalance between these two objectives could affect the reciprocity of interests that explains the partners' desire to work together. For example, one partner, in contrast to another or others, may be interested in extending the geographic coverage of commercial preferences, notwithstanding the cost in terms of limiting other members' depth of commitment. As evidenced in the European case, this may even lead to existential crises in the integration process.

Dissidence among partners at this level may be attributable to multiple factors having to do with their relative size and endowment of power, strategies for participating in the world market, trade policy strategies, or the degree of diversification of their foreign trade. But it could also be attributable to political factors having to do with the foreign policy interests of each of the partners within the surrounding region—for example, South America in the case of Mercosur or Eastern Europe in the case of the European Union—or, in particular, the relations with a major power, such as the United States in the case of Mercosur.

Tension between the objectives of broadening and deepening may occur in relation to the elements that distinguish a voluntary economic integration process among sovereign nations, which are as follows:

- Unlimited access to the markets of the partners, meaning permanent and not precarious access, conceived as a judicially protected right, which does not necessarily fully vest initially but generally requires reasonable time. This includes all goods but may also include services and the remaining factors of production.

- Discrimination with respect to third parties. This is the essence of preferential treatment. It implies differentiating between "us" and "them." This distinction can be made through the common external tariff, with specific rules of origin for goods as well as for services, or with policies regarding the internal functioning of the markets (for example, those pertaining to economic competition, intellectual property, or government procurement contracts).

- A certain level of collective disciplines, understood as restrictions on discretionary, unilateral behavior of the partners. They could be limited to what is necessary to maintain preferences in the reciprocal trade of goods, or they could be extended to the level of foreign trade policies and sectoral policies or even to significant aspects of foreign policy. They always include macroeconomic policies, either implicitly (meaning they presume a minimal degree of de facto coordination of the principles of fiscal and exchange stability) or explicitly (through formal mechanisms for coordination).

The density of the commitments that the partners assume regarding these three elements will vary, depending on whether they decide to integrate their markets in a free trade area, in a customs union, in a common market, or in an economic union. Nevertheless, these conceptual categories are proving insufficient for understanding today's integration processes, from the point of view of international relations. As the North American Free Trade Agreement (NAFTA) and Mercosur demonstrate, elements of one or another category may be combined. A free trade zone may have, as it does in NAFTA, many of its own elements of more advanced forms of integration, especially on the level of policies and tools with respect to the internal functioning of the markets. Or a common market, as Mercosur seeks to become, could eventually have the elements of a highly flexible customs union or perhaps only those of an advanced free trade zone.

In any of these cases, two factors may influence the realization of the objectives of broadening and deepening a voluntary process of economic integration. One is the degree of interdependence among the countries, measured by the size of the flow of trade and investment among the members in relation to what each has with third countries. The second is the degree of polarization of relative power among the partners, measured by the size of the respective markets, the gross domestic product, and their imports. With greater interdependence and multipolarity—the case of the European Union—it seems more feasible to reconcile countries' interests with the objectives of broadening and deepening. If interdependence is less developed, it seems less feasible to attain the objective of deepening; relatively low levels of reciprocal trade, for example, make it difficult to realize ambitious objectives for the integration of markets and economic policies. And when polarization is strong, asymmetrical interdependence may make expansion unnecessary, and deepening might heighten the perception of dependence on a hegemonic power; what may be important in these cases is "insurance against protectionism" for access to the markets of the larger party. Furthermore, these are very dynamic processes, constantly exposed to the changes in the international context, to the domestic changes affecting the partners, and to the actual results of the integration process.

Therefore, the tension between the degree of progress on commitments regarding preferences and in the collective disciplines that are their consequences—deepening—and the question of with which parties one progresses—broadening—can only be understood from the logical perspective of the dynamic of a joint effort among sovereign nations with a relatively wide range of foreign policy alternatives. That range, however, tends to diminish to the degree that the commitments and common disciplines deepen and integration moves closer to the point of no return, a point at which the whole begins to take on an identity beyond that of its parts.

THE BROADENING-DEEPENING
QUESTION AT THE FOUNDING OF MERCOSUR

The idea at the outset of Mercosur was to develop a core upon which something broader and deeper could gradually be built. Apparently, both in 1986, when Argentina and Brazil undertook bilateral integration, and in 1990, when Mercosur became a reality, policymakers had in mind the mistakes and limitations of earlier projects for regional economic integration, specifically the Latin American Free Trade Association (LAFTA) and the Latin American Integration Association (Asociación Latinoamericana de Integración, or ALADI).

It was believed that those experiences were frustrated, among other things, by an excess of member countries, too dispersed and too different—eleven members, which included all of South America and Mexico—and by overly ambitious definitions of commitments: first, the establishment of a free trade zone, and later that of a Latin American common market. The result was an imbalance between the broad geographic territory and the objectives of deepening, which translated into an enormous distance between the rhetoric and formal commitments and their actual impact on trade flows and investors' expectations.

In contrast, Mercosur had far fewer full partners—the four signatories to the Treaty of Asunción—and a limited core of strong commitments: The door was left open for an initial period of five years, ending in November

1997, for the possible entry only of Chile; and only two commitments were binding as of Mercosur's beginning in 1991 (one to a zero tariff within four years, and the second, to be instituted at the end of that term, to a common external tariff).[1]

The potential for broadening and deepening was symbolized in the name: the Common Market of the South. This symbol was not arbitrary but rather loaded with intentions on at least two levels. On one level, *South* could mean either all of South America or all that is south of the Rio Grande. The ambiguity was not just a question of semantics. Rather, the idea was (1) to send clear signals of the vision of the future, leaving aside the implications of the name originally considered for Mercosur (the Southern Cone Common Market, which would have caused problems for northeastern Brazil and would have implied that membership was limited to the countries of southern South America); and (2) to leave entry open after the five-year start-up period to any country in ALADI, which is the political and formal framework within which Mercosur functions.

On another level, the label *common market,* as well as the long-term objective defined explicitly in the first article of the Treaty of Asunción, evokes commitments much more profound than the mere free trade of goods, including that of a customs union. Thus the final direction, in this regard, is clearly plotted. The political commitment of the partners is to a common market. This is what they communicated to their citizens, to investors, and to other countries. This is what they presented to their legislatures and what the legislatures approved.

The methodology of integration employed by those who initially pressed for an alliance between Argentina and Brazil—an alliance that later found its primary expression in Mercosur—seeks to take account of the following:

- The now-frustrated experience of the period one could call "integration fiction."
- The fact that both Argentina and Brazil were still experiencing marked macroeconomic instability and incipient development of their respective experiences in democratic institutionalization.
- The then still-evident sequelae of years of mutual mistrust, especially among their diplomats and significant power groups, such as the armed forces and businesspeople.
- The awareness of the necessity to take a few significant steps with a strong multiplier effect—a common tariff in four years, for example—thus sending clear signals to the markets about the direction of the integration project and its goal of not turning back and producing a new environment in which next steps would be determined.
- The fact that Mercosur would be visualized as a by-product of

domestic transformation of production and competitive entry into the world market. Mercosur's objectives, instruments, and rhythms should therefore be consonant with the same advances achieved domestically. Central elements of such processes included macroeconomic stability and trade liberalization. It was not coincidental that the four-year period for reaching a zero tariff coincided with the opening of Brazil's economy.

When Mercosur was founded, it was accepted that broadening and deepening would be subject to very strict criteria in the initial period and to relatively broad criteria for the indefinite future. For the initial period, a deep focus was given importance, but it was limited to two central commitments: the zero tariff and the common external tariff. The geographic territory was limited to only four countries and possibly one more, Chile. Through these five countries runs a corridor including twenty large cities, from the triangle formed by Belo Horizonte, Rio de Janeiro, and São Paulo in the north to Montevideo, Buenos Aires, and Santiago in the south. This corridor contains some seventy million urban consumers with a per capita income of about U.S.$10,000. From an economic point of view, that corridor is the nucleus of Mercosur's consumption and production.

These considerations were present in two of the central principles that motivated Argentina and Brazil's leap forward in 1990 in building their strategic alliance: creating a regional "habitat" to promote the global competitiveness of their businesses and strengthening their capacity to negotiate international economic relations. The first principle implicitly encompassed the idea of deepening common domestic activities to transform production and attain systemic competitiveness. The second principle also implicitly meant expanding the horizon of such efforts, extending the international projection of companies to markets in the Latin American region, in the Western Hemisphere, and in Europe. Doing so required developing an agenda for negotiations to obtain preferential access to markets in the ALADI nations, the United States, and the European Union. Together with Mercosur's own markets, these three areas represent 80 percent of the international markets of the four partners.

From this point of view, since the beginning of Mercosur the question of broadening has been about more than the incorporation of new partners. It is part of a broader question, that of defining Mercosur's foreign trade policy, which itself extends even to that of the partners' agreement regarding the proposal to create a free trade area from Alaska to Tierra del Fuego. This issue is of special importance to Brazil. It is no exaggeration to say that in June 1990, when Brazil accepted the Argentine proposal to accelerate the establishment of a common market between the two countries, it acceded also to the commitment to participate jointly in the hemisphere-wide negotiations called by the U.S. government. This is reflected in the parallels observed in negotiations on an economic cooperation agreement, signed in December 1990 under the auspices of ALADI, between Argentina and Brazil—the central pillar of the agreements on free trade included later in Mercosur and in the Treaty of Asunción—and the "four-plus-one" agreement with the United States, signed in June 1991.

THE BROADENING-DEEPENING QUESTION
IN THE FIRST YEARS OF THE INTEGRATION PROCESS

More than a decade has passed since the integration process that led to Mercosur began, during which unprecedented experience has been acquired and progress toward initial goals realized. Concurrently, as is to be expected, the national and international context in which the question of broadening and deepening applies has evolved. From the analytical perspective, three qualitative changes have taken place in Mercosur during this period:

- There has been substantial progress in the consolidation of democracy and in transforming production in each of the partners, including each one's opening to international trade.
- Economic interdependence is greater than it was at the beginning of Mercosur, with growth in trade and in reciprocal investments, encouraging developments in transportation and telecommunications, and cooperative projects involving physical infrastructure and energy. Today, hundreds of companies have outlined and established strategies for regionalizing production, trade, and services.
- Public opinion now regards Mercosur as an appropriate way to face the challenges and opportunities of globalization and to forge a regional identity, strengthening the respective national identities.

As for the scope of the commitments undertaken, the period elapsed has allowed the realization, in large measure, of the two main commitments introduced in 1991 by the Treaty of Asunción. The first is liberalizing the trade of goods, which has been achieved in substance. Nonetheless, much remains to be done to consolidate this objective: Exceptions persist, and the large gray area of nontariff restrictions needs to be addressed. Progress has also been substantial toward the second commitment, the common external tariff, but the agenda still pending for consolidation is significant. The customs union is very flexible, with different levels of loopholes and exceptions. The products that have entered the common customs space are still subject to an external tariff upon crossing the border into the customs territory of another Mercosur partner.

It was never stated that the objective of the common market would be fully realized by the end of the established transition period, December 31, 1994. Although the treaty defines its long-term objectives, it includes only prescribable goals with regard to the customs union. This interpretation was endorsed at the Las Leñas Summit in July 1992, when the member countries approved a timetable for the implementation of specific measures that would allow the common market to operate fully by 1995. This goal was essentially reached when Mercosur's Program of Action to the Year 2000 was approved.

Concretely, in these first years, Mercosur has experienced a large part of the simplest phase of generating economic interdependence by eliminating barriers to reciprocal trade and investment. It is gradually entering into the more complex stage of administering interdependence, in which tensions and conflicts generated by the connection of the respective markets and economic systems could feed uncontrollable tendencies toward fragmentation, unless significant progress is made in the institutional aspects of the integration process.

In the current phase, although a customs union has been established, the partners have had difficulty coming to agreement on the common external tariff. Such difficulty has reflected, among other things, speculation within certain Argentine sectors that it might be in their interest to maintain Mercosur as a free trade zone, without the disciplines inherent to a common external tariff. That speculation harks back to the strategy of developing free trade on a hemisphere-wide level, and to some extent it reflected the temptation to follow a model of insertion into the international economy more like that of Chile. In Brazil, this sentiment was perceived as an indication that Argentina was not a dependable partner and that it preferred a special trade relationship with the United States. Moreover, this perception fed tendencies to limit the scope of Mercosur commitments and to elevate the idea of a South American free trade zone.

For different reasons for each partner, the broadening-deepening dilemma seemed headed toward broadening. Finally, however, the Ouro Preto Summit and the approval of the common external tariff helped reestablish the original balance between broadening and deepening. This balance was reaffirmed in 1997 when both governments agreed that broadening could not go forward to the detriment of deepening. During President Clinton's visit to Brasilia and Buenos Aires in October 1997, he conveyed the importance he attributes to Mercosur as an element of regional economic and political stability, and presidents Menem of Argentina and Cardoso of Brazil showed the importance they placed on the deepening of Mercosur as leverage in the hemispheric negotiations for the Free Trade Area of the Americas (FTAA).

In recent years, Mercosur's broadening objectives have progressed prudently, within the restricted guidelines established at the time of its founding, along three fronts. First is the association of South American countries, as expressed concretely through the free trade agreements undertaken with Chile and Bolivia and in a first preferential agreement with the Andean Community. Of course, as the trade liberalization programs that are part of these free trade agreements are carried out, the aforementioned problem with lack of significant differentiation between full and associate membership could arise. This problem could become more intense, insofar as an associate member that does not have to apply the common external tariff may be more attractive than a full member to investors who wish to enter the expanded market, in particular the large Brazilian market. The associate member would then be a free rider, with advantages substantially similar to those of full membership—that is, access to the markets of members—and with none of the costs implied by the collective disciplines derived from the customs union.

The second front that has seen progress concerns the plan of action for establishing a hemispheric free trade area, which was agreed upon at the Miami Summit. At ministerial meetings, particularly the one held in Belo Horizonte, and during the visit of President Clinton, Mercosur's identity and its perseverance as a differentiated system of preferences were reaffirmed. Nonetheless, Mercosur has not yet defined how it will be differentiated as a preferential system within the framework of the FTAA, a hemispheric free trade area. This is one of the pending items on the agenda for the deepening of Mercosur.

The third front concerns the development of transatlantic relations with the European Union. Mercosur has made a point since its inception of highlighting the importance of its relationship with Europe, reflecting the direction of its foreign trade and the origin of direct foreign investment flows. In both cases, European countries account for 25–30 percent of total foreign economic participation in the Mercosur countries. The main event was the agreement on the framework for relations, executed with the European Union in December 1995 in Madrid. In 1996 and 1997 the technical work was undertaken, to culminate in the first half of 1999 at the eagerly awaited European Union–Mercosur summit, which should result in a political agreement on the scope of negotiations on free trade and investment.

During these years, the region has continued to strike a balance between limited broadening and limited deepening. The overriding approach has been to proceed with great caution, in large part to accommodate the progress of Mercosur's evolution with the stabilization and transformation processes of the project's members. As presidents Cardoso and Menem made clear at a bilateral meeting in 1997, Mercosur's broadening will not be achieved at the expense of its consolidation and deepening.

BROADENING VERSUS DEEPENING IN THE FUTURE

Bearing in mind the status of the broadening-deepening issue at Mercosur's founding and during the first decade of the integration process of the region, it is apparent that the future interplay between the objectives of broadening and deepening of Mercosur will depend on three factors:

1. The evolution of the negotiations for free trade in the hemisphere and with the European Union. Both shall continue to be interconnected, because neither the United States nor the European Union would allow their companies to lose their competitive position in Mercosur as a result of a preferential free trade agreement with only one of the two. The European proposal for a free trade agreement with Mexico to make up for ground lost to NAFTA demonstrates this proposition. At the same time, both sets of negotiations will depend on the evolution of the proposal for a "Millennium Round" in the World Trade Organization (WTO). It is quite possible that Argentina and Brazil will continue to see the WTO as the most appropriate forum for advancing on issues concerning trade relations with both the United States and Europe, particularly in agricultural issues. Thus it seems reasonable to predict that preferential and hemispheric or transatlantic free trade agreements would take a back seat to a round of WTO negotiations.

2. The requirements of preserving mutual benefits among partners, especially between Argentina and Brazil. In particular, the noninclusion of services and government procurement in the commitments of Mercosur, or their very limited or insufficient inclusion, could be perceived as a competitive advantage for the Brazilian service companies, especially those in engineering and construction, which already enjoy access to the open markets of the other partners. The lack of deepening of Mercosur on this level could generate pressure to dilute the concept of a customs union and its assimilation in the broader concept of a South American free trade area and—most definitely—in the hemispheric free trade area. Alternatively, accelerated deepening in the area of services and government procurement could stimulate further deepening commitments on other trade and economic policy issues, which would in turn affect noneconomic areas of the integration process. Integration processes then could advance by leaps and bounds, impelling change in the coordination of macroeconomic policies—including addressing the long-standing idea of a monetary union—and in sectoral policies, regarding objectives of the joint transfor-

mation of production and the policies and instruments that foster the systemic competitiveness of the partners.

3. The evolution of some associated countries, especially Chile, into full partners of Mercosur. This evolution will be more feasible if (1) Chile does not enter into NAFTA or a bilateral free trade agreement with the United States and (2) Mercosur's deepening in the area of services and government procurement is not easily extendable to associated countries.

The agenda for the future deepening of Mercosur will nonetheless be very broad. For many issues deepening will be linked to the agenda for consolidation. It comprises the three elements previously discussed that distinguish a voluntary integration process among sovereign nations (unlimited market access, differentiation with respect to third parties, and collective disciplines). In these three areas, much remains to be done for Mercosur to approach the objective of a common market. In the short run, a common regime for the automotive industry, planned for the year 2000, and the sugar industry, for which indirect subsidies are understood to distort competition, should be adopted. But it is also necessary to make progress on effective rules of the game in other areas, especially economic competition and unfair trade practices.

The consolidation-deepening agenda also must address the elimination of artificial asymmetries that persist, affecting the relative competitiveness of companies operating out of one or another partner. These asymmetries originate in governmental policies (tax incentives to investment, for example) or in the practices of companies (for example, unfair trade practices and distortions of the conditions of economic competition).

Deepening Mercosur will mean, in particular, accentuating the active enforcement of collective disciplines among the partners thus curbing their natural tendency to discretionary, unilateral behavior. Macroeconomic policies, foreign trade policies, and sectoral policies are the priority areas of action. Moving forward with deepening measures will require a qualitative leap on an institutional level to equip Mercosur with effective rules of the game—that is, rules that have a real impact. It is a question of economic and political effectiveness. Bearing in mind the asymmetry in market size and the objective of overcoming obstacles to the placement of investments, the perceived precariousness of the rules of the game would limit the benefits of integration to the larger economy of the area but would introduce an element of disruption in the attainment of mutual benefits among the partners. This perceived precariousness might even affect the internal legitimacy of Mercosur in some of the partners and, consequently, the ability to maintain the political sustainability of the integration process.

Perhaps the principal danger Mercosur faces is becoming infected with the so-called ALADI virus, the return to past practices carried out according to the maxim that the rules of the game would be followed to the degree possible. This qualification made the commitments undertaken seem largely precarious. Although there were always good political and economic reasons to explain this precariousness—in general, the pragmatic argument that realities, particularly the frequent economic emergencies, must predominate—investors and businesspeople found it difficult to have faith in the promised broader market.

The idea of easily disposable rules of the game, if found to prevail, may erode the credibility of Mercosur in the eyes of markets, investors, and citizens. If it is believed that the rules of the game are only indicators of desired behavior that, if necessary, could easily be set aside or modified, then political leaders may feel inclined to approve rules with a low effectiveness potential (that is, rules without much effect on reality in the Mercosur organs). They could even be rules with very ambitious nominal objectives, since approving them would not necessarily imply a heavy cost for the member nations.

If Mercosur eventually turns out to be heavy on rhetoric and light on the effectiveness of its rules of the game, the consequences could be calamitous. Political imperatives might impel a premature step toward the free trade commitments agreed upon with the ALADI countries or an easily revocable lowering of tariffs. Such an outcome could reintroduce in Mercosur the idea that timing and the rules of the game can breezily be adapted to short-term realities, thus provoking protectionist demands from sectors or countries that believe they are not in a position to face regional economic competition.

Then neither governments nor businesses would feel bound by Mercosur. Both collective and internal policy discipline—one of the major contributions of international agreements, especially economic integration agreements, to the political and economic culture of the participating countries—would be diluted.

Effectively enforced rules of the game do not have to be a straitjacket on the very dynamic realities of countries in the midst of stabilization and transformation, as some pragmatists assert. It is perfectly possible to reconcile instrumental flexibility with the notion of a rule-oriented process. What is important is that the necessary modifications be introduced based on preestablished—that is, predictable—criteria and procedures. What is required is a methodology of integration that entails effective commitments on a few matters with a large multiplier effect—in other words, few rules on key topics, which are subject to modification only in accordance with preestablished criteria and procedures.

For these reasons, it is in the political realm, ultimately, where the boldest efforts are needed for the deepening of Mercosur, and these efforts are all the more necessary as the agenda for external negotiations increases in complexity. Some of those efforts might well be directed toward the gradual creation of common institutions that promote a shared vision as the process of integration advances, the reciprocity of interests among partners, and the resolution of trade disputes brought about by increasing economic interdependence. The need for this institutional strengthening will be even more urgent if Chile joins Mercosur.

The question of the relationship between the objectives of broadening and deepening need not be an intractable dilemma. One objective need not be attained at the expense of the other. In the framework of open regionalism, conceived as an instrument for the transformation of production and for competitive entry in the global markets, consistent with WTO commitments, this relationship is more a question of methodological efficiency. Political vision, institutional quality, dynamic maintenance of the framework of mutual benefits, and appropriate management of time frames are the keys to attaining this methodological efficiency.

NOTES

1. The four-year term for achieving a zero tariff was later extended for a few more years for products deemed sensitive. The common external tariff was defined at a summit in Ouro Preto in 1994.

5

Establishing an Industrial Policy for Mercosur

Ricardo Markwald & João Bosco Machado

Almost a decade after the signing of the Treaty of Asunción, the Common Market of the South (or Mercosur) is, from the standpoint of trade, a resounding success. During this period trade with non-Mercosur countries has doubled, expanding at 12.1 percent per year—above the world average—while trade within Mercosur has quadrupled. In 1997, intraregional trade flows were estimated to account for one-quarter of exports and more than one-fifth of the imports of the expanded market, fostering a significant degree of interdependence among the economies of the four member countries (see Table 5.1).

Mercosur stands out as the first Latin American integration project to achieve a reasonable degree of success, after more than three decades of frustrated efforts. Even in the broader context of the world economy,

Table 5.1 Intraregional Trade in Mercosur, Selected Years

	1991	1993	1995	1997	Growth, 1991– 1995	Percent per Year, 1991– 1997
Exports						
Total (millions of U.S. dollars)	45,896.0	54,122.0	70,029.0	82,900.0	11.1	10.4
Within Mercosur (percentage)	11.1	18.5	20.5	24.9	29.6	26.3
Outside Mercosur (percentage)	88.9	81.5	79.5	75.1	8.1	7.3
Imports						
Total (millions of U.S. dollars)	34,264.0	48,082.0	79,859.0	96,650.0	23.6	18.9
Within Mercosur (percentage)	15.3	19.6	18.1	21.4	28.9	25.7
Outside Mercosur (percentage)	84.7	80.4	81.9	78.6	22.5	17.4

Source: Comtrade Database, United Nations Statistical Division (UNSTAT).
Note: Figures for 1997 are estimated.

Mercosur represents an auspicious and original experience with the formation of a midsize economic bloc made up of economies not yet fully developed.

The rapid expansion of trade among the economies of Mercosur and the high level of participation of industrialized products in the trade flows within the bloc—much higher than in extraregional exports—are some of the outcomes that justify a positive assessment of the project to integrate the Southern Cone. Paradoxically, those same factors—that is, reorientation of trade so as to favor the members of the bloc and the prominent participation of capital-intensive goods in intraregional exports—provoked just the opposite assessment in a polemical World Bank study written by Alexander Yeats.[1] In fact, consistent with findings from that study, discriminatory tariff preferences and sectoral policies are the factors that explain the increase in exports within the bloc, as well as their high degree of concentration in products for which Mercosur has no comparative advantage, as shown by their low share in extraregional exports. If that were the full story, Mercosur would seem to be a worrisome case of diversion of trade.

Most critics of the World Bank study, however, have suggested that in order to examine the static effects stemming from integration (that is, the balance between creation and diversion of trade), it would have been more accurate to look at the members' imports, not exports. When viewed from this angle, Mercosur gives rise to few concerns. Imports from other Mercosur countries have expanded at a higher rate than imports from outside the area (see Table 5.1), but this differential is much less than that found in the export trade, and even that is reduced significantly when crude oil imports are excluded (oil imports were redirected to favor intraregional suppliers). Even for the automotive industry, considered by critics of Mercosur to be the paradigmatic example of diversion of trade, extraregional imports grew at rates close to those of imports among the Mercosur countries.[2] Indeed, it should be noted that in the ranking of importing countries drawn up by the World Trade Organization (WTO), Argentina ranks first among economies with the greatest growth rates in the 1990–1996 period, and Brazil placed sixth, just after China.[3] The fantastic pace of the trade opening in the Southern Cone countries—not the diversion of trade fostered by Mercosur—is what merits special attention.

The integration project set out precisely to exploit economies of scale and gains in productive specialization as well as to use the regional market as a platform for the more competitive insertion of the Mercosur economies into the global scene.[4] Mercosur's success, then, must be measured against these goals as well. The paper by Yeats may be misdirected, but he did raise two important issues: (1) the existence of major differences in the patterns of trade within and beyond the bloc and (2) the need for more systematic, rigorous monitoring of the presumptions regarding the dynamic advantages of the integration process. (These matters should have been of special concern to those throwing in their lot with the benefits of the creation of the regional bloc.)

These concerns run through the two sections that follow. In the first we describe the differences in the patterns of exports within and beyond the bloc and examine how they have evolved since Mercosur was founded, with a view to identifying possible changes.[5] In the second we highlight the role a community industrial policy could play to better exploit the dynamic advantages of the integration process.

TRADE PATTERNS IN EXPORTS WITHIN AND BEYOND THE ZONE AND INDUSTRIAL TRADE WITHIN MERCOSUR

Between 1992, the first year after the signing of the Treaty of Asunción, and 1996, intraregional exports grew by 23.9 percent per year, three times greater than exports to the rest of the world. Tables 5.2 and 5.3 portray this evolution using two types of classification. Classification in Table 5.2 combines origin by sector (primary, semiprocessed, and manufactured products, highlighting in the first two the natural resource base of the goods), capital and labor intensity in the use of the factors, and the sources of international competitiveness of the different types of products (economies of scale, productive specialization, and intensity in R&D [research and development] spending). Table 5.3, also covering only exports, breaks down industrialized products according to the degree of technological intensity of the exported products. The technological content is determined by the relationship between spending on R&D and the value of production in each sector.

In 1996 Mercosur exports displayed three reasonably defined, differentiated patterns. The first corresponded to exports among the member countries (that is, intraregional flows) and exports to the Latin American Integration Association (ALADI) countries (including Mexico); the second had to do with exports to the North American Free Trade Agreement (NAFTA) countries; and the third, more of a mixed bag, reflected exports to the European Union, the Asian countries, and the rest of the world.

There is a striking similarity between exports among the Mercosur countries and their foreign sales to the ALADI countries, which accounted in the aggregate for more than 30 percent of Mercosur exports in 1996. In both cases commodities and semiprocessed goods together accounted for approximately 43 percent of total exports, and manufactured goods accounted for 56 percent of export flows. A closer look also reveals few differences between these two markets. Exports to ALADI included a larger share of primary energy products (crude fuels) and manufactured goods

Table 5.2 Exports from Argentina and Brazil, by Groups of Goods, 1992, 1996 (percent, unless otherwise noted)

Groups of Goods	1992 Mercosur	ALADI	NAFTA	EU	Asia	Other	Total	1996 Mercosur	ALADI	NAFTA	EU	Asia	Other	Total	Growth 1992–1996 (average annual percentage) Mercosur	Extra-Mercosur
Primary Products	18.0	10.6	16.6	30.6	26.3	17.9	22.0	22.1	22.0	16.9	31.2	25.9	20.7	23.8	30.3	9.7
Agricultural	15.1	8.8	12.0	22.7	12.3	13.5	15.6	13.0	9.2	11.0	24.6	15.7	16.4	16.0	8.5	9.6
Mining	1.9	0.7	1.7	7.9	14.0	4.2	5.6	1.4	0.9	2.4	6.6	9.9	4.0	4.4	16.0	3.3
Energy	1.0	1.1	2.9	0.0	0.2	0.2	0.8	7.7	11.8	3.5	0.0	0.3	0.3	3.4	107.1	40.2
Industrialized Goods	81.9	89.3	83.3	69.3	73.7	77.6	77.4	76.8	76.2	80.1	67.6	72.7	69.1	73.4	21.9	6.2
Semiprocessed	19.6	19.1	25.0	44.7	31.8	46.0	33.5	21.1	20.7	21.8	44.6	45.3	49.1	34.3	26.2	9.3
Agricultural-labor intensive	7.2	10.0	12.2	31.3	13.9	26.8	19.3	10.1	12.3	10.0	34.4	27.3	28.8	21.3	35.1	11.4
Agricultural-capital intensive	3.1	2.4	3.5	4.7	4.0	11.5	4.9	3.4	2.8	5.1	4.6	5.6	15.3	5.9	26.2	14.5
Mining	5.1	4.7	5.5	7.2	13.9	2.8	6.7	4.6	4.4	4.7	5.8	12.3	3.3	5.7	20.8	3.8
Energy	4.2	2.0	3.8	1.5	0.1	4.9	2.6	3.0	1.3	2.0	0.6	0.1	1.7	1.5	13.9	−12.1
Manufactured	62.3	70.2	58.3	24.6	41.9	31.6	43.9	55.7	55.5	58.3	23.0	27.4	20.3	39.1	20.5	3.2
Labor intensive industries	9.7	8.5	22.1	8.5	4.5	5.3	10.1	8.4	8.1	17.8	8.4	5.5	4.9	9.0	19.3	4.7
Industries intensive in economies of scale	34.2	36.4	15.5	8.2	30.5	18.7	20.5	29.5	25.6	18.7	6.6	16.7	8.8	17.1	8.0	0.0
Specialized suppliers	13.0	18.5	11.2	4.3	3.9	6.1	8.4	12.5	13.4	12.9	5.1	3.4	5.4	8.5	22.7	6.6
Industries intensive in R&D	5.4	6.8	9.5	3.6	3.0	1.5	4.9	5.4	8.4	8.9	2.9	1.8	1.2	4.5	23.8	4.9
Other	0.1	0.1	0.1	0.1	0.0	4.5	0.7	1.1	1.8	3.0	1.1	1.4	9.9	2.7	—	7.6
Total	100.0	100.0	100.0	100.0	100.0	100.0	100.0	100.0	100.0	100.0	100.0	100.0	100.0	100.0	23.9	
Exports (billions of U.S. dollars)	6.45	5.09	8.78	14.72	6.76	6.62	48.44	15.21	6.80	11.74	17.37	10.69	9.75	71.56		
Share (percentage)	13.3	10.5	18.1	30.4	14.0	13.7	100.0	21.3	9.5	16.4	24.3	14.9	13.6	100.0		

Source: Data are from the Secretariat for Foreign Trade in Brazil and the Instituto Nacional de Estadística y Censos (INDEC) in Argentina.
Note: ALADI includes Mexico and excludes the Mercosur countries. NAFTA excludes Mexico.

Table 5.3 Exports of Industrialized Goods from Argentina and Brazil, by Technological Intensity, 1992, 1996

Degree of Technological Intensity	1992							1996							Growth, 1992–1996 (average annual percentage)	
	Mercosur	ALADI	NAFTA	EU	Asia	Other	Total	Mercosur	ALADI	NAFTA	EU	Asia	Other	Total	Mercosur	Extra-Mercosur
Low	31.2	36.0	54.0	68.2	68.2	68.7	56.4	31.4	41.4	54.7	74.2	71.8	76.0	57.8	22.2	8.2
Low-average	26.6	25.5	19.6	16.3	21.5	18.3	20.5	26.0	24.5	19.1	12.9	17.2	13.8	18.8	21.2	2.3
Average-high	39.7	35.5	16.6	12.1	7.8	12.1	19.1	39.6	28.5	16.1	10.0	10.3	9.3	19.4	21.8	2.5
High	2.5	3.0	9.8	3.4	2.5	0.9	4.0	3.0	5.6	10.1	2.9	0.7	0.9	3.9	27.5	5.6
Industrialized Goods	100.0	100.0	100.0	100.0	100.0	100.0	100.0	100.0	100.0	100.0	100.0	100.0	100.0	100.0	21.9	6.2

Source: Data are from the Secretariat for Foreign Trade in Brazil and the Instituto Nacional de Estadística y Censos (INDEC) in Argentina.
Note: ALADI includes Mexico and excludes the Mercosur countries. NAFTA excludes Mexico.

with a high R&D component as compared with exports among the Mercosur countries, which were concentrated more in agricultural commodities and manufactured goods that take advantage of economies of scale. Otherwise, the pattern of exports to the two markets was quite similar (see Table 5.2).

Exports from Mercosur to NAFTA disclose a surprise: The profile of exports to that market, which accounted for 16 percent of Mercosur's external sales in 1996, did not differ dramatically from the pattern of exports among the Mercosur countries or exports to ALADI. External sales to NAFTA did show, however, a smaller concentration in commodities, especially energy exports, and a slightly higher share of manufactured goods, especially labor-intensive manufactured goods (footwear, manufactured leather goods, textiles, wooden furniture, and so on). The relative participation of semiprocessed goods was identical to the level of exports among the Mercosur countries and in the trade flows with ALADI.

An entirely different export profile was characteristic of the flows to the countries of the European Union, Asia, and the rest of the world, which together accounted for just over 50 percent of Mercosur exports. In these markets, the relative share of exports of manufactured goods (23 percent on average) was less than half of what one finds in the flows of exports within Mercosur and to NAFTA and ALADI. Furthermore, the share of agricultural commodities and semiprocessed agricultural goods was two or three times higher in exports addressed to the European Union, Asia, and the rest of the world than in sales to the countries of ALADI and NAFTA and in trade flows among the Mercosur countries.

The differences in the regional profile of Mercosur's exports become even clearer when examining the technological content of exported industrial manufactures, shown in Table 5.3. In flows of exports to the European Union, Asia, and the rest of the world, industrial goods with low technological content had a very high level of participation—near 75 percent, on average, of the exports of industrial manufactures in 1996. The predominance of agricultural goods in the export flows to those markets, together with the low technological sophistication of the industrial goods, described a markedly traditional export pattern. NAFTA occupied an intermediate position, as nearly 55 percent of the purchases of industrial goods from Mercosur had a low technological content. With its purchases of aircraft produced by Brazil, NAFTA was the leading market for Mercosur's high-tech exports, but the overall technological profile of exports to NAFTA was nonetheless qualitatively lower than one finds in the flows among the Mercosur countries or in Mercosur exports to the ALADI countries. This characteristic and the greater presence of labor-intensive manufactured goods in sales to the NAFTA countries are what distinguish exports to NAFTA from those to other countries of the Americas.

Finally, in comparing exports among the Mercosur countries with exports to the ALADI countries, one notes the higher technological profile of the industrial manufactures traded among the Mercosur members. The discrepancies, however, are insufficient to distinguish separate patterns for these two markets.

As the foregoing analysis demonstrates, an "export pattern" is sensitive to both the geographic breakdown of exports and the classification of flows based on alternative typologies. For the specific case of Mercosur, the simple opposition of patterns, one for the Mercosur countries and another for trade with non-Mercosur countries is, in fact, quite inadequate. The profile of exports among the Mercosur countries differs little from that which prevails in the Mercosur-ALADI trade flows. Furthermore, the Mercosur-NAFTA flows reveal a pattern clearly differentiated from the other trade flows with non-Mercosur countries, such as those with the European Union and Asia. Tariff preferences and discriminatory sectoral policies, factors highlighted by Yeats to contrast the profile of exports within and beyond Mercosur, are insufficient explanations for that variation.[6]

Indeed, what is most striking when comparing the structures of trade among the Mercosur countries from 1992 to 1996 is the difficulty of identifying a clear "Mercosur effect." The key changes in this time span had to do with the increase in the exports of primary energy products and, to a lesser extent, of labor-intensive, semiprocessed agricultural goods; accompanying that increase was a reduction in the relative share of exports of manufactured goods in general, especially of manufactured goods that rely heavily on economies of scale. Contrary to what Yeats suggested, those changes appear to reflect a certain skewing of export patterns among the Mercosur countries to the primary sector. Yet the explanation is much simpler: The increase in the share of trade accounted for by primary energy commodities has to do exclusively with the explosive increase in fuel exports from Argentina to Brazil, which is also observed in Argentina's trade with ALADI and NAFTA countries. This increase resulted mainly from deregulation of the sector, replacement of liquid fuels by natural gas, and privatization of the Argentine state-owned oil enterprise Fiscal Oil Fields (Yacimientos Petrolíferos Fiscales, or YPF). In other words, more than a Mercosur effect, the increased trade in primary energy products was a change wrought by the process of structural reform in the Argentine economy and the resultant record-setting pace of production in the Argentine energy sector.

In addition, as shown in Table 5.3, the technological profile of exported industrial goods among the Mercosur countries remained constant from 1992 to 1996, whereas the profile of industrial exports to non-Mercosur countries deteriorated slightly.

The foregoing observations lead to a troublesome conclusion: The dynamic advantages that integration should supposedly foster take shape very slowly, if at all. The pattern of exports among the Mercosur countries changed little over four years, despite vigorous growth in total volume, and the small increase in extraregional exports elsewhere does not point to an improved insertion of Mercosur into the world economy in either quantitative or qualitative terms.

That conclusion bears examination from the standpoint of another indicator, the index of intraindustry trade, which tracks both exports and imports of goods in an industrial segment. Consistent with international experience, the gains from intraindustry trade are significant because the companies tend to specialize in a few lines of production, thereby bolstering their productivity and efficiency. Greater specialization results in greater international competitiveness, which is one of the anticipated effects of the regional integration process.

Table 5.4 shows the intraindustry trade index for 1992–1996, distinguishing between intra-Mercosur trade flows (strictly speaking, bilateral flows between Brazil and Argentina) and trade flows with non-Mercosur countries (trade flows of Brazil and Argentina with selected trading partners).[7] The evolution of intraindustry trade flows within Mercosur as shown in that table is more encouraging than results from the preceding analysis. In 1996 the indicators were at a reasonably high level, revealing the existence of a mature pattern of trade among the members of the bloc. More important still, the indexes display a stable or upward trend over time.

The same cannot be said for trade with non-Mercosur countries. Except for trade with ALADI countries, the intraindustry trade indicators are low in every instance and even show a downward trend. In transactions with the ALADI countries, intraindustry trade is stable and indicators reasonably high only for chemical products, although indicators point to sustained growth for the mechanical equipment and transportation sectors, which is explained mainly by the trade in electrical machinery and highway vehicles.

In sum, though attenuated in the case of intrabloc trade, the conclusion remains that the establishment of Mercosur and advances in the regional integration process have yet to promote a significant difference in member countries' insertion into the world economy.[8] It could be argued that it is too soon to expect the full flowering of Mercosur's potential, yet perhaps a more skeptical position is in order, considering that Mercosur's success is premised upon the automatic operation of processes that involve a drastic reworking of the industrial structure. That is the point of view that undergirds the policy suggestions in the following section.

Table 5.4 Intraindustry Trade Index for Mercosur Members and Trade Partners, 1992–1996

Trade Within Mercosur (bilateral trade, Brazil-Argentina)

SITC[a]	Description	1996 trade		Intraindustry trade indicator				
		Value (billions of U.S. dollars)	Share (percent)	1992	1993	1994	1995	1996
5	Chemical and related products	1.16	9.8	61	46	50	57	62
6	Manufactured goods classified by raw material	1.68	14.1	17	22	27	42	46
7	Mechanical and transportation equipment	4.14	34.7	41	58	65	73	66
8	Other manufactured articles	0.43	3.6	36	29	33	60	62
5 to 8		7.41	62.2					
0 to 9		11.93	100.0					

Mercosur[b]-ALADI Trade

SITC[a]	Description	1996 trade		Intraindustry trade indicator				
		Value (billions of U.S. dollars)	Share (percent)	1992	1993	1994	1995	1996
5	Chemical and related products	1.29	11.5	53	48	48	55	55
6	Manufactured goods classified by raw material	2.29	20.4	19	21	24	29	33
7	Mechanical and transportation equipment	2.46	22.0	24	27	32	44	50
8	Other manufactured articles	0.61	5.5	57	55	49	47	44
5 to 8		6.66	59.4					
0 to 9		11.21	100.0					

(Continues)

Table 5.4 Continued

Mercosur[b]-NAFTA Trade

SITC[a]	Description	1996 trade		Intraindustry trade indicator				
		Value (billions of U.S. dollars)	Share (percent)	1992	1993	1994	1995	1996
5	Chemical and related products	4.35	15.0	39	34	28	24	23
6	Manufactured goods classified by raw material	4.38	15.1	30	34	29	34	27
7	Mechanical and transportation equipment	10.63	36.5	44	45	41	37	39
8	Other manufactured articles	3.12	10.7	18	19	16	17	15
5 to 8		22.48	77.3					
0 to 9		29.10	100.0					

Mercosur[b]-EU Trade

SITC[a]	Description	1996 trade		Intraindustry trade indicator				
		Value (billions of U.S. dollars)	Share (percent)	1992	1993	1994	1995	1996
5	Chemical and related products	4.71	12.5	44	32	29	28	26
6	Manufactured goods classified by raw material	4.97	13.1	38	33	38	40	32
7	Mechanical and transportation equipment	12.16	32.2	36	29	24	22	22
8	Other manufactured articles	2.19	5.8	28	25	27	23	21
5 to 8		24.03	63.6					
0 to 9		37.78	100.0					

(Continues)

Table 5.4 Continued

SITC[a]	Description	Mercosur[b]-Asia Trade						
		1996 trade		Intraindustry trade indicator				
		Value (billions of U.S. dollars)	Share (percent)	1992	1993	1994	1995	1996
5	Chemical and related products	1.44	7.0	43	38	41	43	44
6	Manufactured goods classified by raw material	4.19	20.3	8	11	11	13	14
7	Mechanical and transportation equipment	6.04	29.4	17	20	12	14	13
8	Other manufactured articles	1.93	9.4	18	19	19	15	16
5 to 8		13.60	66.1					
0 to 9		20.57	100.0					

Source: Basic data from the Secretariat for Foreign Trade in Brazil and the Instituto Nacional de Estadística y Censos in Argentina.

Note: ALADI includes Mexico and excludes the Mercosur countries; NAFTA excludes Mexico. The intraindustry trade indicator is the Grubel and Lloyd index, calculated based on SITC-Rev. 3, in the breakdown to three digits.

a. SITC = Standard International Trade Classification.

b. Corresponds to trade of Argentina and Brazil.

BASES FOR AN INDUSTRIAL POLICY FOR MERCOSUR

Not only has the growing integration of the regional markets among the countries of Mercosur not yet produced significant changes in patterns of trade with the rest of the world, but the long-term objective of establishing a full-fledged customs union in the region could be compromised unless the member countries achieve greater convergence in competitiveness among the productive structures of the economies. So far, negotiators have neglected efforts to attain that convergence among their respective industrial policy instruments. Given the open nature of the integration process, the convergence of industrial policies could be an effective instrument for industrial restructuring and reconversion and help define a type of international insertion based on dynamic comparative advantages.

Asymmetry in size and competitiveness of the economies of the Mercosur countries has two effects when intraregional trade barriers are eliminated: (1) It alters the product listing of the firms through mergers and associations, and (2) it gives rise to changes in the location of industry within the region, unless uniform industrial policies even out the levels of competitiveness. A liberal foreign trade regime should be accompanied by an industrial policy that creates the conditions for a permanent change in already-established comparative advantages.

Proceeding on these premises, an evaluation of the main obstacles that stand in the way of implementing a community industrial policy in Mercosur is called for. It is first necessary to discard a nonpolitical course of action. The fiscal constraints faced by Argentina and Brazil have become one of the main stumbling blocks to implementing industrial development policies at the regional level. Although in recent years Brazil has implemented active industrial policies, Argentina's economic situation led to the gradual abandonment of the state's historic role in fostering competitiveness in industry. In principle, the option of adopting the current Argentine model is incompatible with the objective of building the foundations for permanently boosting regional competitiveness. If another sort of integration is sought, one based only on static comparative advantages, the risk is high that integration would be weakened and difficult to sustain in the long run, considering the differences in efficiency among the economies of the region.

Thus, at this stage of consolidation of the customs union, the debate on implementation and the management style of industrial policy in Mercosur should shift to the regional level. Given the integration agenda, it would not be advisable for Mercosur's member countries to preserve their autonomy regarding instruments for industrial promotion and restructuring or to disregard the spillover effects on their partners arising from measures taken on a strictly national basis.

So what form should industrial policy in the region take? The process of consolidating a customs union in Mercosur has uncovered several challenges that regional industrial policy must address:

- Preserving comparative advantages in those sectors important to the pattern of international insertion of the Mercosur economies.
- Restructuring or productive reconversion of those sectors with declining productivity or those negatively affected by the regional integration process, in light of the differences in productivity among the installed capacity in the Mercosur countries.
- Creating comparative advantages in fields opened up by the operation of the expanded market, especially for sectors whose products have greater technological content and greater dynamism in international trade.

These three challenges ultimately define a multifaceted approach that gives direction to the implementation and management of industrial policy.

Maintaining comparative advantages should be seen as the result of preserving an open trade regime with respect to third countries, such that the competitive pressure generated by imports forces permanent improvement in the efficiency of the tradable goods sector. What is desired in this case is the efficacy of "passive restructuring," whereby the government refrains from eliminating market failures or externalities to ensure competitiveness, relying instead on microeconomic initiatives induced by the risk that imports might displace locally manufactured goods or by the fear of losing the market share in international trade.

Passive restructuring should include elimination of the whole set of barriers responsible for the reduction in sources of competition. This means, in large part, the implementation of foreign trade policy that keeps protectionism low and competition policy that uses state purchasing power as instruments for promoting a competitive, open environment in Mercosur. It is a question of preserving competition within the unified market and of creating competitive pressures by opening the regional market to foreign trade. This strategy should bolster industrial competitiveness and force firms to strive to steadily improve their efficiency and their products' quality.

The introduction of industrial restructuring or reconversion policies in the community will necessitate a hard look at the economic efficiency and political feasibility of such measures. If the development of the customs union proceeds as expected, the trade creation effect will be greater than the trade diversion effect. Whenever industrial restructuring policies are proposed as part of a regional integration program, the question of how to manage trade diversion is brought into the discussion. Evidently, the broader the scope of the restructuring policy, the lesser the trade creation effects resulting from the regional integration process. As argued by Jacob Viner, the formation of a market free from barriers to the circulation of merchandise will bring gains in well-being so long as the less efficient local production is replaced by the more efficient regional supply.[9] The result will be the elimination of the least efficient poles of production and increased regional concentration of supply in those sectors where significant differences in productivity exist among the various local industries.

Although this outcome is desirable from the standpoint of efficiency in the allocation of resources, often the economic impact of the integration process on the affected sectors and countries can produce political pressures to keep barriers to intraregional trade in place or to replace tariffs with nontariff barriers, for example. This is especially so when economies are asymmetric, as they are in Mercosur. An effective regional restructuring policy thus requires a clearly defined set of mechanisms and a program of assistance targeting specific industrial sectors in order to minimize pressures to limit trade liberalization.

Industrial restructuring policy should not only aim to provide selective and temporary protection to specific sectors but also to encourage a reduction in installed capacity and the relocation of firms as a means of adjustment. However, there is no doubt that the dismantling and reconversion of national productive apparatuses might be warranted if restructuring cannot ensure that a specific segment of industry will become competitive enough to participate in a customs union that lacks obstacles to intraregional trade. The necessity for such a measure stems from past reliance on import-substitution and sectoral support policies in the countries of the region, which postponed the adjustments industry needed to make to become competitive and improve general well-being and income distribution, while at the same time it diverted considerable public funds from investment in social sectors and infrastructure development.

In general, the participation of the Mercosur countries in international trade is limited to sectors with little dynamism (that is, those in which world demand is not on the rise) and to exports of products with low technological content. According to many analysts, these limitations indicate a gap between the performance of firms in the regional market and that of cutting-edge firms located elsewhere. That disparity results from the interaction of at least three factors: (1) the scant involvement of the producers in the local markets in technological activities, (2) the absence or inadequacy of resources and institutional mechanisms to support local research and development activities or to improve national systems for innovation, and (3) deficiencies in educational preparation for the workplace, especially in training for technical personnel and scientists.

Despite state sponsorship or other encouragement of technological development activities—which is inherently characterized by a high concentration of resources, sectoral selectivity, and high risk, and which has been historically provided by the states more or less explicitly—externalities in that area suggest that it is one of the fields in which so-called market failures are most clearly manifested. The set of guidelines, policies, and instruments responsible for promoting technological development activities nationally constitutes the framework for what is called *technology policy*.

The debate on the role of technology policy in shaping the pattern of international insertion of Mercosur economies and in determining the long-term direction of development has always been controversial among economists who, depending on their theoretical bent, attribute one weight or another to the roles of the state and the market as agents that promote technological development. According to the adherents of liberalism, the direction of a country's technological development depends on the local conditions of production (that is, on the relative endowment of local factors and the price ratios among them); technology changes when the prices of the factors of production do. Those conditions of production and the policies on technology, investment, and foreign trade that affect them together determine the capacity of the system to obtain access to the new technologies. From the regulatory standpoint, open trade and elimination of restrictions on direct foreign investment are the instruments through which countries get access to the new technologies: Countries can purchase capital goods that incorporate state-of-the-art techniques, and they can protect the investments of transnational firms that are able to, in effect, transfer new goods and productive processes to the national economy. According to this view, the state should work to improve the educational system, which translates into a better-trained labor force and higher productivity and wages.

Advocates of the interventionist approach believe that the role of the state is inestimable in orienting and promoting technological development and that that role is not diminished under a liberal economic regime. The United States, cited by liberals as an example of the efficacy of the market mechanism vis-à-vis the state, provides counterevidence, according to the interventionists, that there has been no successful technology policy without extensive state intervention. In the national system of innovation of the United States, public spending by the federal government financed 50–70 percent of total spending in the economy after World War II, with the largest share going to private-sector R&D. The concentration of spending on R&D in segments of industry that produce goods and services for the military defense system yielded major technological externalities, which are thought to be essential for the competitiveness of high-tech sectors of the U.S. economy, such as the civil aeronautics and computer industries.[10]

The discrepancies between liberal and interventionist positions point to the pressing need to examine the timing, conditions, and efficacy of adopting mechanisms for technology policy that will ensure a gradual improvement in technology and a better pattern of insertion of Mercosur economies into the world market. Discouragement with Brazil's scanty success with attempts to develop a national system for innovation and with the short-term nature of its economic policy measures aimed at macroeconomic stabilization has turned technology policy into a nonissue for the Mercosur countries. Nonetheless, the integrated market presents opportunities and windows for pooling efforts or drawing on the specific advantages of particular countries, or both, to produce community synergies in support of technological development.

In Mercosur, the scarcity of resources (mainly financial) for restructuring production and for technological development is one of the major obstacles to implementing regionwide policies for industrial promotion. Here the difficulties are on two levels. The first, which is structural, stems from the high indebtedness of the states and the fiscal crisis of the Mercosur countries. Finding the financing for programs to restructure industry and for technological training that can establish a secure trajectory for making investments—and thus enable long-term, sustainable growth of the community market—depends on the success of the stabilization policies now in place and on the alleviation of fiscal constraints. The second difficulty is related to the institutional apparatus of Mercosur. The Treaty of Asunción does not define any mechanism or fund for financing regional programs for restructuring and reconversion of industry and technological development. One way to deal with this problem might be to use a fraction of the fiscal revenues collected from import taxes (after the common external tariff is in place) to set up an industrial promotion fund.

The first priority of a community industrial policy could be to establish a regional fund for the restructuring of production. The asymmetries in size among the countries of the region imply widely disparate levels of competitiveness between large-scale industries and industries in the small economies. Active policies for restructuring and reconversion can help assure that remaining obstacles to regional trade will eventually be eliminated. It is also necessary to improve regional infrastructure, which will require massive investment, especially in transportation. The Fonplata (Financial Fund for the Development of the River Plate Basin), created in 1974 to finance the promotion of economic development and physical integration in the region, could be the first step toward establishment of a regional fund for restructuring and investment in infrastructure. In 1996 the Fonplata approved just two projects, both for Argentina, for a total of U.S.$13.4 million. Although the volume of loans made in 1996 surpassed that for the previous year by about 40 percent, the amount of financing requested by the countries of the region annually outstrips the amount available in the fund. In December 1996 the ministers of the Mercosur countries concluded that Fonplata's operations should be brought up to standards for a financial institution designed to serve the requirements of the integration process.

Obviously, then, for all the reasons discussed in this section, the negotiating agenda for the integration of Mercosur must include consideration of the convergence of industrial policies. Mercosur has already changed the competitive environment: The market has expanded, and the liberalizing direction that trade policies have taken since the mid-1980s has been reaffirmed. The strategies for competition adopted by the firms, industries, and countries in Mercosur are being implemented in this new context and therefore should take stock of the impacts of the formation of the regional market on the sustainability of the local productive arrangements.

There is no doubt that political consensus, transparent administration, and stability of the instruments for industrial policy are essential to Mercosur's viability. Without them, the integration project could not create fair conditions of competition among the various countries and thus establish an environment in which barriers to the free movement of goods are eliminated and trade is open in relation to third countries. Yet complementary efforts are needed in this stage of Mercosur's consolidation. The working agenda must aim to attain greater convergence of regulatory policy, with macroeconomic policy, trade policy, and industrial promotion foremost. Harmonization of these policies is vital, as it is for the methodology for addressing the asymmetries. In sum, it is time for the debate on implementation and management style of industrial policy to shift to the regional level.

NOTES

1. Alexander Yeats, "Does Mercosur's Trade Performance Raise Concerns About the Effects of Regional Trade Arrangements?" policy research working paper 1729, World Bank, Washington, D.C., 1997.

2. Miguel Rodríguez Mendoza, "Afinal, que Mercosul é este?" *Revista Brasileira de Comércio Exterior* 50 (1996) (Rio de Janeiro, Fundação Centro de Estudos do Comércio Exterior).

3. World Trade Organization, *Focus Newsletter* (Geneva: World Trade Organization, 1997).

4. Yeats expressed skepticism with respect to the dynamic advantages fostered by integration and cited Omar N. Toulan and Mauro F. Guillén: "Some claim that trading blocs can serve as a testing ground for eventual global integration as they allow firms to gradually develop internationalization skills. In many ways this argument is similar to the infant industry protectionist argument in which barriers are used to protect domestic industries until they develop the skills necessary to compete internationally. Unfortunately, such policies have a fairly poor record in Latin America. The same potential fate could lie in store for firms operating under the protection of Mercosur, in which their level of competitiveness is confined to the demands and pressures of the Mercosur market, rather than the global one.

While it is too early to tell whether firms are in fact viewing Mercosur as a launching pad, interviews held with managers do not reveal that they are in fact doing this" (Yeats, "Does Mercosur's Trade Performance Raise Concerns," p. 31).

Devlin was more confident, yet cautious: "Export learning curves are an extended process rather than an event that can be measured in the first few years of Mercosur's existence. The truth of the matter is that in this more dynamic context the determination of comparative advantage is a very complicated task" (Robert Devlin, "Em Defesa do Mercosul," *Revista Brasileira de Comércio Exterior* 50 [1997] (Rio de Janeiro, Fundação Centro de Estudos do Comércio Exterior), 26.

5. The statistical information in the first section concerns the two leading partners in Mercosur, Argentina and Brazil. Uruguay and Paraguay are omitted only because the foreign trade databases for these two countries were unavailable.

6. Yeats, "Does Mercosur's Trade Performance Raise Concerns."

7. The intensity of intraindustry trade is usually measured using the Grubel and Lloyd index. That index is a coefficient that ranges from 0 percent to 100 percent and indicates the proportion of intraindustry trade in relation to the total marketed in a given industrial segment. When imports correspond exactly to exports in the same productive activity, the coefficient is 100 percent, whereas in the absence of intraindustry trade, it is equivalent to 0 percent. It is generally acknowledged that there is intraindustry trade in those cases in which the index takes on values greater than 40 percent and displays stability over time. In addition, the intraindustry trade index is generally calculated only for sections 5 through 8 of the Standard International Trade Classification (SITC).

8. Similar conclusions, from an exclusively Argentine perspective, are presented in recent papers: Marta Bekerman and Pablo Sirlin, "Patrón de especialización y política comercial en la Argentina de los 90," *Desarrollo Económico* 36 (1996) (Buenos Aires); Marta Bekerman and Pablo Sirlin, "Los desafíos de la política industrial en el Mercosur," *Revista del Centro de Estudios Bonaerenses* 63–64 (February–March 1997); Horacio Cepeda, "Un análisis de la composición de las exportaciones argentinas" working paper, Instituto de Desarrollo Industrial, Buenos Aires, 1997; Bernardo Kosakoff, "Business Strategies and Industrial Adjustments: The Case of Argentina," working paper 67, Economic Commission on Latin America and the Caribbean, Buenos Aires, 1996.

9. Jacob Viner, *The Customs Union Issue* (New York: Carnegie Endowment for International Peace, 1950).

10. James M. Utterback and Albert E. Murray, "The Influence of Defense Procurement and Sponsorship of Research and Development on the Development of the Civilian Electronics Industry," working paper 77-5, MIT Center for Policy Alternatives, Cambridge, Mass., 1977.

6

Mercosur's External Trade Negotiations: Dealing with a Congested Agenda

Roberto Bouzas

The implementation of the Common Market of the South (Mercosur) has been accompanied by a demanding agenda of external trade negotiations. This agenda included a renegotiation of preexisting preferential agreements with other members of the Latin American Integration Association (ALADI) and participation in preparatory negotiations for a Free Trade Area of the Americas (FTAA) and for a preferential trade agreement with the European Union (EU).

The incentives to engage in these ambitious negotiating exercises were twofold. One was the imperative to redefine Mercosur member states' relations with other ALADI partners to prevent a perforation of the common external tariff (CET) formally adopted in January 1995. The other was largely reactive. In effect, participation in preparatory negotiations for an FTAA and for a Mercosur-EU preferential trade agreement can be best understood as a response driven by exogenous events. Although the governments of the four Mercosur member states adhered to the 1994 Miami commitment to negotiate and start implementation of an FTAA by the year 2005, enthusiasm was far from homogeneous. As in a domino game, the Miami commitment gave impetus to the conclusion of a framework agreement with the European Union.

In this chapter I review the external trade negotiations of Mercosur after the creation of the customs union. The first section deals with intra-ALADI negotiations. The second one reviews Mercosur's role in the preparatory phase of FTAA negotiations and identifies some key issues for the future. The third section briefly discusses the content and rationale of the interregional agreement signed with the European Union. The final section presents some conclusions.

MERCOSUR AND THE
LATIN AMERICAN INTEGRATION ASSOCIATION

Before the establishment of the customs union, each Mercosur member country was part of the network of bilateral preferential arrangements under the umbrella of ALADI. Since Mercosur agreements were themselves part of ALADI, Mercosur relations with other ALADI members was an issue from the very beginning. In particular, the Treaty of Asunción (1991) left the door open for the future accession of any ALADI member to Mercosur after a five-year waiting period. An exception was set for ALADI members that were not party to a subregional agreement (a clause tailor-made for Chile). By the end of the transition period for Mercosur member countries (December 31, 1994), all preexisting bilateral preferential arrangements were to be terminated and replaced by new, "multilateral-ized" preferential agreements.[1] To proceed into these negotiations, envisaged to lead eventually to free trade agreements, Mercosur member countries agreed on a set of negotiating guidelines in 1994.[2]

Although on aggregate the "rest of ALADI" (which excludes Mercosur) takes less than 10 percent of total Mercosur exports, trade relations between Mercosur and the rest of ALADI are far from negligible. In particular, "rest of ALADI" markets are of considerable importance to some Mercosur members, such as Argentina. In 1997 the value of Argentine exports to the rest of ALADI was 60 percent greater than the value of exports to the United States, contributing 12 percent of total Argentine sales abroad.[3] Moreover, the rest of ALADI is the second major outlet for Mercosur manufactured exports after the customs union itself.[4] These facts, jointly with Mercosur membership in ALADI, gave the multilateralization negotiations high priority.

The Chile-Mercosur Free Trade Agreement

In June 1996, after two years of negotiations, Mercosur signed its first free trade agreement (FTA) with Chile.[5] The Chile-Mercosur FTA includes a commitment to gradually and automatically eliminate all tariffs. One of the peculiarities that distinguish this FTA from other preferential arrangements in Latin America is the absence of permanent exemptions to the liberalization program.[6]

The Chile-Mercosur agreement also prohibits the implementation of new trade restrictions and commits the parties to identify and dismantle nontariff barriers (NTBs). The agreement includes a rules-of-origin regime drafted after Mercosur's and establishes a dispute-settlement mechanism. Goods subject to special import regimes (excluding those shipped from free trade zones) will enjoy the benefits of the agreement for a maximum of five years. The Chile-Mercosur FTA was accompanied by a parallel protocol on physical integration, which confirms Argentine and Chilean commitments to make coordinated investments in road infrastructure.

The Chile-Mercosur agreement was not easy to negotiate. Although the Chilean economy is fairly open, its agricultural sector (particularly temperate-zone agriculture) remains highly protected. Overcoming the opposition of Chilean agricultural producers in the temperate zone to an FTA with Mercosur was thus a difficult task. The balance was tilted by strong support from other potential beneficiaries, mainly manufacturing and service-producing industries with large export potential to the enlarged market.[7] Foreign policy considerations also played a role in the official decision to overcome the stiff opposition raised by domestic agricultural interests.

On the other side of the table, the smaller Mercosur partners were unenthusiastic about an FTA with Chile. Having paid the price of a relatively high CET for domestically nonproduced goods (such as capital goods), the smaller economies found few incentives to support an agreement that would erode their preferences in the larger markets. However, the priority given to the issue by the Argentine government, plus Brazilian authorities' readiness to go along, left the smaller parties with few options but to follow.

The reasons behind Argentine official enthusiasm with an FTA with Chile were based on economic, strategic, and political grounds. The economic rationale was to increase the potential for trade interactions and to facilitate access of Argentine products (particularly those of regional economies) to Pacific ports and markets (hence the importance attributed to the parallel agreement on physical integration). But there were at least three other strategic and political reasons: First, to tighten bonds with a neighboring country with which Argentina had been close to war less than a decade earlier; second, to build a critical mass to counterbalance Brazil's weight and influence in Mercosur; and third, to lay the basis for concerted action in the FTAA process on the part of Chile and Mercosur. The FTA with Chile served Mercosur an additional purpose: It set the framework for future negotiations with other ALADI member countries.

The Bolivia-Mercosur Free Trade Agreement

In December 1996, one year after the plurilateralization of preexisting bilateral preferences, Bolivia and Mercosur also entered into an FTA. The Andean Community (AC) gave Bolivia a special waiver to engage in bilateral negotiations with Mercosur. As in the Chile-Mercosur agreement, the FTA with Bolivia included several schedules for tariff elimination. About 95 percent of the total tariff schedule—representing an estimated 80 percent of total effective trade—will reach free trade in a period of ten years.

The remainder will enjoy 100 percent preferences for a maximum of fifteen years. Bolivia was granted a list of nearly twenty "especially sensitive" products (mainly sugar and oilseeds), which will reach free trade only after eighteen years. The Bolivia-Mercosur FTA also included agreements on normative issues such as NTBs, rules of origin, safeguards, and dispute-resolution mechanisms. A protocol on physical integration was also signed.

For Bolivia, the FTA with Mercosur will enable domestic producers to circumvent the negative discrimination that stems from the formation of the customs union. The share of Mercosur markets in total Bolivian exports reached 15 percent in 1997, with total export values only 30 percent below Bolivian sales to the rest of the AC. For Mercosur, the importance of the FTA with Bolivia does not rest on trade values. Bolivia is a small trade partner, although it will turn into a major natural gas exporter to Brazil by the turn of the century. For Mercosur, the agreement served to regularize trade relations with Bolivia and to constitute the second step toward building a network of consistent FTAs throughout the region. This network may eventually lead to the formation of a South American Free Trade Area (SAFTA).

Negotiations with the Andean Community and Mexico

As demonstrated by negotiations with the Andean Community, however, the building of a SAFTA will not be a smooth process. Initially, talks with the AC were delayed because of its lack of definition as to whether talks should proceed group to group or follow a four-plus-one scheme similar to that adopted with Bolivia and Chile. The impasse was aggravated by the temporary suspension of Peru's membership in the AC. Eventually, as the AC countries decided to go ahead with group-to-group negotiations, differences on substantive issues emerged.

The AC and Mercosur have stood apart on several issues. Mercosur's stance has been to refuse permanent exemptions, as it had done already in the FTAs signed with Bolivia and Chile. Both parties also broke ranks on the length of the list of especially sensitive products: Mercosur favored a short list after the precedent set by the Chile-Mercosur and the Bolivia-Mercosur FTAs, whereas the AC was inclined to a larger number. The debate on "temporary exemptions" (so-called encapsulated products) and on the length of the list of especially sensitive products touches the wider issue of preferential treatment to less-developed countries. Mercosur has refused to endorse this principle, one long honored by ALADI (and its predecessor, the Latin American Free Trade Association) and the AC.

Negotiations also stalled on issues such as rules of origin, export processing zones, and treatment of the agricultural sector. For the AC, Mercosur rules of origin (the same ones that still apply to intraregional trade and govern the FTAs with Bolivia and Chile) are too restrictive to allow domestic producers to reap the benefits of a preferential agreement.[8] Similar differences prevailed for the treatment of export processing zones and agriculture.

The reconciliation of these divergent interests has been made more difficult by intra-Mercosur differences about what would be an acceptable agreement. For some Mercosur member countries, particularly Argentina and Uruguay, relegating agricultural products (a sensitive sector for the AC) to a later phase in the liberalization process would make the deal unattractive. Such an agreement would bring few benefits in terms of improved market access in the short term, yet at the same time erode their (and Paraguay's) preferential access to the large Brazilian market. By the same token, the Andean countries with the largest industrial sectors (particularly Colombia) feared that an FTA with Mercosur might expose their industries to increased competition from abroad and erode intra-AC preferences. The weight of the case is illustrated by the rapid growth of Colombian manufactured exports to Venezuela in recent years.

Mercosur and the AC also failed to reach a less ambitious agreement to multilateralize preexisting bilateral preferences.[9] Eventually, in April 1998 the AC and Mercosur reached an agreement to negotiate and implement a fixed-preferences "multilateralization" agreement by October 1998 and to negotiate and implement an FTA as of January 2000. However, the first of these deadlines was not met, and it is uncertain whether future targets will be met. If a Mercosur-AC free trade agreement is eventually negotiated, it is likely to resemble those already signed with Chile and Bolivia. There are several reasons for this. First, a radically different agreement would negatively affect the credibility of Mercosur. Second, it would be hard to convince all Mercosur member countries that extra-Mercosur partners are entitled to receive more favorable treatment than that granted to custom union members. Finally, the AC may feel mounting pressure to sign an FTA if some of its member countries find it increasingly attractive to follow the Bolivian four-plus-one path.[10]

Negotiations between Mercosur and Mexico have been less ambitious but have faced equally difficult obstacles. At the political level, relations between the two parties soured after Mexico refused to extend to other ALADI members the benefits granted to its partners in the North American Free Trade Agreement (NAFTA).[11] Mercosur has not offered to sign an FTA with Mexico. Rather, its stance has been to first renegotiate preexisting bilateral agreements, including the issue of compensations. So far, the parties have failed to reach a mutually satisfactory deal. On the one hand, as in the case of Mercosur-AC negotiations, the "historic patrimony" includes sensitive products; on the other, the structure of supply of the Brazilian and Mexican economies is competitive, which mobilizes domestic opposition to a trade liberalization agreement. The issue is further complicated by the fact that costs and benefits of market access concessions would be unevenly distributed within Mercosur. Mexican demands to include automobiles, telecommunications products, and information systems in a new agreement mean that Brazil would make the most significant market access concessions. In contrast, freeing agricultural trade would benefit Mercosur's smaller partners the most.

Trade negotiations with Mexico have posed tough challenges for the process of shaping a common trade agenda. Results have been mixed, as demonstrated by the fact that in December 1997 the four member countries decided to act independently in regard to preexisting bilateral agreements with Mexico. Although Brazil let bilateral preferences fade away, Uruguay extended them for an additional year. Argentina and Paraguay also rolled preferences over, subject to the initiation of negotiations about compensations.

MERCOSUR AND HEMISPHERIC TRADE NEGOTIATIONS

In the Summit of the Americas held in Miami in December 1994, the presidents and chiefs of state of thirty-four countries of the Western Hemisphere agreed to negotiate a regionwide free trade area by the year 2005. The decision was followed by intense preparatory activity, which included four trade ministerial meetings held in Denver, Cartagena, Belo Horizonte, and San José and multiple exchanges in the context of twelve working groups. So far this process has served to collect a significant amount of comparable quantitative and qualitative information on trade flows and trade regimes throughout the hemisphere. In April 1998, on the occasion of the second presidential summit in Santiago, the heads of state formally launched negotiations.

All Mercosur members shared the commitment to implement a hemispheric free trade zone by the year 2005, but enthusiasm varied widely.[12] Although there was an attitude of warm support in Argentina, the smaller economies were largely indifferent. The Brazilian government, in turn, was openly reluctant. The reasons are easily understood.

For Paraguay and Uruguay, economic integration in the subregion was already demanding the bulk of public and private actors' energies and attention. The hemispheric process was thus perceived as relatively distant from the daily demands of membership in Mercosur.

Brazilian reluctance rested on several grounds. For one thing, although the largest Mercosur partner stands to gain the most from free and more stable access to the U.S. market, its diversified economic structure also means that transition costs from trade liberalization vis-à-vis the United

States would be sizable. Moreover, since Brazil has a diversified regional trade pattern and relatively high protection, a hemispheric preferential agreement—and particularly an agreement with the United States—would involve a large potential for trade diversion. Finally, owing to the nature of domestic regulations and the stage of the economic reform process, Brazilian authorities are not inclined to make reform commitments that go beyond those already made in the context of the World Trade Organization (WTO), especially in new, nonborder issue areas.

The Argentine authorities seemed initially the most enthusiastic about the FTAA process. The reasons were lower anticipated transition costs, "expectational" considerations (such as lock-in effects and lower country-risk premiums), and the positive influence that the hemispheric agenda was expected to have on Mercosur's own intraregional negotiations.

Yet national positions have tended to converge since the Miami Summit, owing to several factors. First, the rapid growth of intraregional trade has led the smaller partners (particularly Argentina) to appreciate the mercantilist benefits of having preferential access to the large Brazilian market. Second, as the negotiating agenda became more evident, a more balanced assessment of costs and benefits could be made not only by public sector officials but also by private parties. Finally, as preparatory talks gained momentum and the chances that the U.S. administration would obtain fast-track negotiating authority from Congress diminished, the costs of a recalcitrant and obstructionist position on the part of Mercosur increased, whereas its benefits were considerably reduced.

From the standpoint of Mercosur, at least four broad issues will merit special consideration as negotiations develop following the Santiago Summit: (1) the scope of the FTAA, (2) its implementation, (3) the distribution of costs and benefits of economic integration, and (4) the macroeconomic effects of the FTAA.

The Scope of the FTAA

The experience of more than four years of preparatory talks suggests that the scope of the FTAA will be controversial throughout the negotiations. Although protection at the border is still relatively high in most of Latin America and the Caribbean, the attractiveness of preferential agreements for U.S. negotiators rests on WTO-plus commitments,[13] particularly regarding domestic regulations and nonborder issues such as trade in services, protection of intellectual property rights, treatment of foreign direct investment, competition policy, government procurement, and labor and environmental standards. In effect, the main incentive for the United States to enter into FTAs with Canada and Mexico was to reach "deeper understandings" on issues still uncovered or inadequately covered—as far as the United

States was concerned—by multilateral rules.[14] Many of these WTO-plus issues are sensitive ones for Mercosur member countries. In the majority of them the customs union has not even reached the stage of a shared regulatory approach at the subregional level, even less of a common negotiating stance.

Moreover, some of the issues that remain high on Mercosur's priority list, such as agricultural subsidies and enforcement of U.S. trade remedy laws, are unlikely to be adequately dealt with in either a hemispheric or a bilateral context, as already demonstrated in NAFTA. These divergences do not necessarily pose unsurmountable obstacles to successful completion of negotiations, which will aim precisely at bridging them, yet they do point up areas that will demand considerable energy on the part of the participants.

Implementation of the FTAA

The Miami declaration established the year 2005 as the limit for concluding FTAA negotiations and implementing the agreement. According to the "single undertaking" principle, all commitments would be implemented simultaneously and as a single package—that is, nothing would be agreed upon until all was agreed upon. This formula was designed to ensure a deal as balanced as possible in an environment structurally characterized by large asymmetries of size and power.

Yet the single undertaking commitment was later complemented by that of an "early harvest." The early harvest principle makes reference to interim agreements that may be enforced in areas where consensus among participants prevails. These dual principles may generate tensions if differences emerge regarding the extension and opportunity of such early harvest.

Again, nothing precludes implementation of certain commitments prior to 2005 if all parties find that mutually beneficial. Yet in the context of an uneven playing field, the process by which agreement on an early harvest is eventually reached will be a key issue.[15]

Distribution of Costs and Benefits

The historical experience with economic integration suggests that there are at least two approaches to dealing with the asymmetric distribution of costs and benefits stemming from economic integration among widely different partners. Each approach is dependent upon the degree of trust instilled in the market's ability to produce convergence as opposed to polarization among regions with sizable differences in per capita incomes.

The EU has given an explicit role to the compensation of asymmetries to prevent the consolidation of vicious circles of stagnation and deterioration in disadvantaged regions. This is the role of structural funds and other widely used redistributive mechanisms. NAFTA, in contrast, has paid little attention to these issues, instead emphasizing the role of domestic policies to counterbalance centrifugal forces in a dynamic path of adjustment.

The economies of the Western Hemisphere are characterized by large disparities in size, structure, and level of development. For this reason, the balanced distribution of costs and benefits will necessarily turn into a major issue. A balanced distribution certainly goes beyond special treatment for the smaller economies, which has been the dominant approach so far—to little avail indeed.

Macroeconomics and the FTAA

Although trade policy is largely related to resource allocation, the macroeconomic implications of trade liberalization can hardly be neglected. Moreover, since the WTO-plus agenda fostered by U.S. negotiators goes well beyond border barriers and trade in goods to include issues such as capital market liberalization, the macroeconomic implications of FTAA negotiations may be even more significant.

In recent years Mercosur member countries have made remarkable progress toward macroeconomic stability, yet considerable uncertainty remains about its sustainability and vulnerability to changes in the external financial environment. The economies of the region are still heavily reliant on foreign savings, which makes them vulnerable to volatile capital flows. Moreover, the nominal exchange rate has played a key role in bringing about price stability, raising questions about its sustainability in a less forthcoming international financial environment.

In this context, differences are likely to arise on whether far-reaching trade liberalization can be dealt with independently of issues such as capital-account liberalization ("sequencing"), exchange rate regimes, or the establishment of contingent credit facilities to deal with an unexpected liquidity crisis.

MERCOSUR AND THE EUROPEAN UNION

As already stated, the Miami Summit gave impetus to the signature of a framework agreement between the European Union and Mercosur. The Interregional Framework Agreement signed in December 1995 created an institutional mechanism to carry forward a regular policy dialogue among the two regions but included no specific commitments about trade liberalization. In order to enter into the agreement, Mercosur satisfied the EU's demand to obtain formal recognition under international law.

So far the agreement has mainly served as a vehicle for exchanging information. The bulk of the activity has been concentrated on organizing and identifying the main issues of the interregional trade and trade policy agenda. Signatory countries have not yet agreed on a time frame for starting negotiations on trade liberalization. If the Miami commitment is to be given credence, the EU-Mercosur agenda is still behind that of the FTAA.

The EU interest in an agreement with Mercosur rests on the relevance of the latter as a trade and investment partner. It is likely that strategic considerations raised by the Miami Summit also played a role in the EU's decision to foster closer cooperation with Mercosur. Evolution of the FTAA is thus likely to set the pace of EU-Mercosur negotiations.

For Mercosur, maintaining a balanced approach to North America and Europe makes both political and economic sense. The European Union is a large trade partner—in many cases more important than the United States—and a main source of foreign direct investment. Mercosur thus has an obvious interest in not discriminating against the EU.

Nevertheless, as in the case of the FTAA process, a trade liberalization agreement with the European Union would demand overcoming a difficult agenda. A free trade area limited to industrial products would be unattractive to Mercosur (and probably contrary to the spirit, if not the words, of the WTO's Article XXIV), whereas inclusion of agriculture would be conflictive from the EU's standpoint. However, as international commitments and the dynamics of the EU's widening force reform of the Common Agricultural Policy of the EU, common ground may expand. In any case, progress in substantive negotiations between Mercosur and the EU is likely to be slow.

CONCLUSIONS

Since its formal establishment as a customs union, Mercosur has faced a diverse set of extraregional trade negotiations. Although negotiations with other ALADI members were largely a by-product of the decision to implement a common external tariff, Mercosur's participation in the FTAA process and the signature of an interregional framework agreement with the European Union were largely reactive and driven by defensive considerations. These multiple arenas posed Mercosur with the challenge of developing a common negotiating stance and designing a consistent framework to carry the negotiations forward.

Mercosur's stance has been influenced by its history and structural configuration. Four factors stand out. The first one is that Mercosur included no permanent exemptions to intraregional free trade. This fact has left little room to negotiate noncomprehensive FTAs with other ALADI members. The second factor is Mercosur's intergovernmental structure, which has favored arbitrage among divergent national interests rather than identification and pursuit of a "common interest." The third factor is changing national perspectives and rising trade interdependence within the region, which have stimulated a convergence of national positions over time. The fourth derives from the shared identity of the Mercosur countries—mainly Argentina and Brazil—as a peripheral group of global traders, which makes their interests best served by a strong and well-functioning multilateral trading system.

These factors help explain the results and characteristics of Mercosur's FTAs with Chile and Bolivia and the difficulties faced by the negotiations with the Andean Community and Mexico. Similarly, they account for Mercosur's largely reactive negotiating stance vis-à-vis the FTAA and the European Union. Incidentally, Mercosur's insistence on similar agreements with all South American ALADI members may help bestow some rationale to the patchwork of bilateral preferential agreements that have proliferated throughout the hemisphere since the mid-1980s. Since this structure has the potential to create inefficiencies and increase transaction costs, Mercosur may end up having a positive role in fostering liberalization and transparency in the region, even if a South American Free Trade Area never materializes.

In hindsight, Mercosur's main accomplishment in the FTAA process has been to contribute to making that process a negotiating exercise rather than a framework for extending NAFTA to the rest of the hemisphere. This outcome was certainly facilitated by the U.S. administration's lack of fast-track negotiating authority, which inhibited U.S. negotiators from forcefully pushing their own agenda ahead. In turn, negotiations with the European Union have advanced at the pace set by the FTAA process and are likely to continue to do so.

NOTES

1. The negotiations to "multilateralize" existing bilateral preferential agreements were not concluded before the end of the transition period as originally envisaged. Consequently, since January 1995 preexisting bilateral agreements have been rolled over. The first multilateralization agreement was signed with Bolivia in December 1995.

2. The guidelines proposed (1) multilateralization of preexisting bilateral preferences; (2) minimum generalized preference margins of 40 percent for the remainder; (3) definition of an automatic and linear tariff-cutting chronogram; (4)

definition of a list of temporarily exempted products and a phaseout calendar; (5) definition of a list of sensitive products to receive below-minimum preferences (30 percent) for three years (after which they would be included in the general liberalization program); (6) agreements on rules of origin, safeguards, dispute resolution, duty-free zones, customs valuation, export incentives, special customs regimes, harmonization of technical and sanitary standards, and unfair trade practices; and (7) automatic extension of benefits negotiated with third parties.

3. In 1997 the value of Argentine exports to Chile was similar to the value of total Argentine sales to the U.S. market. Although these indicators provide a static picture of trade intensity, they illustrate the structure of existing trade flows.

4. In recent years Brazilian manufacturing exports have grown almost exclusively in regional markets.

5. Chilean authorities decided not to join Mercosur for several reasons, including Mercosur's initially low credibility, a flat import tariff rate, and the expectation of an early accession to the North American Free Trade Agreement (NAFTA). The Chile-Mercosur free trade agreement was formalized as an "economic complementation agreement" under ALADI's umbrella.

6. Tariff cutting will proceed according to four schedules, namely: (1) a general list with a 40 percent initial preference margin and 100 percent preferences in eight years; (2) a list of sensitive products with a 30 percent initial preference margin fixed for three years and 100 percent preferences in ten years; (3) a list of special sensitive products with no preferences for a period of three years and 100 percent preferences in ten years; and (4) a list of highly sensitive products that maintain their tariffs for a period of ten years and reach 100 percent preferences in fifteen years. Chile also obtained special treatment for wheat and wheat flour, which will reach 100 percent preferences only after eighteen years.

7. Chilean exports to Mercosur include a relatively high share of higher value-added manufactures (such as printing and publishing, chemical products, metal products, and transport equipment). For further details on the Chile-Mercosur FTA, see Manuel Agosín and Roberto Alvarez, "La asociación entre Chile y el Mercosur: Costos y beneficios de un año de funcionamiento," *Informe Mercosur* 3 (July–December 1997) (Buenos Aires, Inter-American Development Bank/Institute for the Integration of Latin America and the Caribbean).

8. Since the CET is still not fully in force, all intra-Mercosur trade remains subject to origin requirements. For certain products Mercosur rules of origin include a double criteria of change in tariff classification and 60 percent of regional value added. Other products are subject to specific requirements. A large share of the Andean Community tradable output (particularly manufactured products) would not meet a 60 percent value-added rule of origin.

9. One of the principles of intra–Latin American trade negotiations has been to preserve the so-called historic patrimony, that is, preferences granted in past negotiations. In the case of Mercosur–Andean Community negotiations, some products subject to preferential treatment by one of the parties are sensitive to others or have turned sensitive in the original country itself; an example is Venezuela's treatment of dairy imports from Uruguay.

10. If Mercosur eventually signs with the Andean Community an FTA radically different from that with Bolivia, the latter may demand parity. Although Bolivia has already signed an FTA with Mercosur, it is formally participating in the negotiations as a member of the Andean Community. The key to a Mercosur–Andean Community agreement may lie in Brazilian-Venezuelan relations.

11. Article 44 of the Montevideo (ALADI) treaty established that Mexico

would extend these benefits to ALADI members. The article was eventually modified to establish that the parties would negotiate compensations.

12. For a discussion of the structure of incentives in Mercosur, see Roberto Bouzas, "Las relaciones comerciales Mercosur–Estados Unidos: Elementos para una agenda minilateral," *Serie Documentos de Trabajo* 4 (1994) (Buenos Aires, Instituto del Servicio Exterior de la Nación); and Pedro da Motta Veiga, "El Mercosur y el proceso de construcción del ALCA," *Integración y Comercio* 1 (September–December 1997). For a broader discussion, see Roberto Bouzas and Jaime Ros, "The North-South Variety of Economic Integration: Issues and Prospects for Latin America," in *Economic Integration in the Western Hemisphere,* ed. Roberto Bouzas and Jaime Ros (Notre Dame, Ind.: Notre Dame University Press, 1994).

13. The WTO-plus agenda includes issues and commitments beyond those addressed and agreed upon at the World Trade Organization.

14. NAFTA even included an explicit link between trade sanctions (through the removal of market access benefits) and enforcement of domestic labor and environmental standards.

15. For a broader discussion on the relevance of the issue of FTAA's architecture, see Luis Jorge Garay, "Regionalismo abierto e integración en las Américas," in *Regionalización e integración económica: Instituciones y procesos comparados,* ed. Roberto Bouzas (Buenos Aires: Editorial Nuevohacer, 1997).

7

Mercosur and the European Union: From Cooperation to Alliance?

Wolf Grabendorff

To understand Mercosur's evolving relationship with the European Union (EU), one must look at a new phenomenon in international relations: biregional relations, with all their strengths and weaknesses. There is little agreement among analysts of international relations about whether, globally, there is movement from bilateral to multilateral and then on to biregional relations within the restructuring of the international system. The most likely scenario is a combination of all three, depending on a shifting definition of national or regional interests.

There is, however, definitely agreement that biregional relations are a European or, better, an EU invention.[1] They are characterized by the need to harmonize different interest profiles from countries and sectors in each region. That usually implies a cumbersome coordination mechanism, or a variety of such mechanisms on different levels, in which the outcomes of negotiations are by no means predictable, partly because the numbers of actors multiply and partly because intraregional agendas are used for domestic political purposes. Moreover, interregional agendas often clash with bilateral and multilateral articulation of interests.

It often seems more difficult to reach an intraregional consensus than an interregional one; one can identify a good number of examples from the EU experience over time. That leads to the assumption that what remains is often the lowest common denominator, which some actors tend to see as a negative rather than a positive outcome for the region's position, depending obviously upon their own stakes in interregional cooperation.

EU-Mercosur relations offer probably the best example of the challenges that arise when a biregional relationship is under construction. These relations are the first formalized agreement between two custom unions, facilitated by a common view of basic societal values and of the international system at large. It is, therefore, also a good example of the ongoing restructuring process within the post–Cold War international system. Both regions share the view that it is necessary to create new alliances in the process of rapid globalization. They also have a common understanding that such new alliances will be principally dominated by leadership from the private sector and formed through the management of the integration processes on both sides. Both regions agree that it is not military might, but financial, economic, and technological management that is in the forefront of the process of economic bloc building and that such management cannot be separated from new political realities, which will be reinforced by the only ongoing bloc-to-bloc negotiations between the EU and Mercosur.

Such a new form of international relations creates also a different form of diplomacy, increasingly involving nonstate actors such as multinational enterprises, political parties, professional organizations, and nongovernmental organizations. The capacity of intergovernmental (as is the case with Mercosur) versus supranational mechanisms (the EU works with both) to manage integration processes and negotiations inside as well as between economic blocs has by no means been decided. Since integration mechanisms are different, not only for historic and geographic reasons but also because of the genesis of their development, a high degree of flexibility might be called for when seeking an adequate institutional framework. At any rate, the establishment of conflict-solving mechanisms, which guarantee the rules of the game within and between integration processes, seems to be the most likely candidate for supranational organs in the near future.

Given that biregional relations have to overcome internal as well as external opposition, it is no surprise that they are and will be fairly vulnerable. Partly this is because many of the benefits will become apparent only in the long term, whereas, like the integration processes themselves, biregional relations incur immediate costs with few immediate benefits for at least some countries and sectors involved on each side. In addition, some external actors, such as the United States, might not find the interregional relationship attractive. The United States might feel excluded from the benefits of such a relationship, especially once a free trade zone between the EU and Mercosur is established. The United States might also find the increase in bargaining power of its junior partners on both sides of the Atlantic quite worrisome. There can be no doubt that the United States would prefer bilateral arrangements with each of the economic blocs in a New Transatlantic Marketplace (NTM), on the one hand, and a Free Trade Area of the Americas (FTAA) agreement that includes Mercosur, on the other. Although the FTAA process is already under way, even without "fast track" in the United States, the NTM is an initiative created within the framework of the "transatlantic dialogue" and was only recently approved by the European Commission; but it has not yet been accepted by the European Council, mainly because of opposition from France.

THE BASIS OF THE EU-MERCOSUR DIALOGUE

The evolving relationship between the two integration mechanisms is based on a hierarchy of political as well as economic assumptions, which also serve as guidelines for the integration process on both sides. The first one is that integration should not be driven by threats. It could be argued that the history of European integration would hardly have been as successful as it has been without the communist threat that existed from the late 1940s to the late 1980s. And one could even argue that in the case of Mercosur, the political decision to end Argentine-Brazilian rivalry—similar to that taken in Europe to end Franco-German distrust—had to do with the conviction that, alone, neither country could very well withstand the challenges of globalization and would have difficulties in becoming a major political actor. Nevertheless, the concept of voluntary association is of great importance to all integration processes, as it has been expressed too by the concept of open regionalism in Latin America. Another point of basic agreement can be found in the absence of value discussions, be those values human rights, the rule of law, democracy, market economy, or the social responsibility of the state. Certain core values can be taken for granted. In part, the shared experience of political dictatorship in Europe and in South America has helped diminish the need for extensive debate about core values that has become so prominent a feature of the dialogue between the EU and the Asian states.

A third point is the willingness of both blocs to accept diversity internally, as well as externally, which leads to the pragmatic assumption that they see each other mutually only as partial partners and not as all-encompassing allies. In assuming their global responsibilities, both partners have also found common priorities with regard to safeguarding regional stability, contributing to peacekeeping and arms control, and collaborating increasingly on environmental issues as well as fighting the drug-related problems.

The willingness of Mercosur to join "the Western Club" and play by its rules also has to be seen in the context of the historical and cultural relations between the Southern Cone and Europe. The strong links that continued over time through the migration of Spaniards, Italians, British, Germans, and Poles in the nineteenth century and up to World War II, or even directly after it, have certainly contributed to the strengthening of the European outlook in many of the Southern Cone countries.

Consider São Paulo's status as the biggest German industrial city anywhere, with over twelve hundred German firms; the extensive presence of French and Italian enterprises in Mercosur; and the increasing economic role of Spain in the last couple of years: All this has made European investment stock in the Mercosur countries by far the most important one.[2]

Although in the 1990–1996 period Europe was only second in foreign direct investment flows, in 1996, thanks to sustained growth in British, French, and Spanish direct investments, the EU was once again Mercosur's most important foreign investor; it has also had a higher growth rate for investments than the United States since the beginning of the 1990s.[3] The EU is Mercosur's first trade partner, even though trade flows are somewhat asymmetric because Mercosur countries are buying a great deal more in the EU than vice versa. When looking at each region's economic interests in the other, it becomes evident how strong the basis for the EU-Mercosur dialogue has become.

THE STRUCTURE OF INTERESTS OF BOTH PARTNERS

For many years, the EU has been seen principally as an economic actor in the world scene with what little political clout it has restricted principally to the wider European context, including Eastern Europe and the Mediterranean. Yet the EU has had long-standing political dialogues with Central America, the Rio Group, the Asian countries, and the Gulf states as well as the very specific transatlantic dialogue with the United States. Nevertheless, the EU has been considered by many as a regional and not a world actor. One could go as far as to see EU-Mercosur relations as one of the expressions of the EU's willingness to change exactly that, from the EU's own perception, misguided impression. The EU wants to be a world actor—and not only economically—and seems to be willing to use its economic muscle and its advanced integration as two major tools to seek further recognition for its new role. In that respect, the interest of the EU in entering an association with Mercosur is to demonstrate its alliance capacity with what now (after the recent Southeast Asian crisis) seems to be the most important emerging market. Its interests also lie in the need to conserve and advance the European economic presence in the region, because any North American Free Trade Agreement (NAFTA) expansion, or FTAA conclusion, might have dramatic consequences for EU trade, as Mexico's NAFTA accession has already demonstrated (the participation of the EU in Mexican foreign trade was halved between 1994 and 1997).

Given the success of Mercosur as the fourth largest integrated market (after the EU, NAFTA, and the Association of Southeast Asian Nations [ASEAN]), with a gross domestic product stronger than China's and an average growth rate of 3.5 percent in the last six years, the EU sees enormous possibilities for further strengthening its economic relations with that region and over time also with current or future associated members of Mercosur. Guaranteed access to such a dynamic market is for the EU of greatest importance, as it is for Mercosur in its relations with the EU. A rapidly increasing flow of trade, aid, and investment from the EU to Mercosur is also seen as of special importance to the EU's well-being, since "current economic growth in the EU is not sufficiently strong to maintain the desired level of employment and income growth rates."[4]

In fact, since 1990 Mercosur has been by far the region that has grown fastest as an export market for the European Union. Comparing the figures from 1990 through 1997, exports to Mercosur grew annually by 19.7 percent, whereas exports to all of Latin America grew by only 12.5 percent and exports to Mexico grew by only 6.3 percent (see Table 7.1). Even if one compares all extra-EU exports, one finds an annual growth rate of only 7.7 percent over that time period, which means that European exports to Mercosur have grown almost three times as fast as extra-European exports to the entire world. From 1990 through 1997, the growth of EU exports to Mercosur was 156 percent higher than the growth of EU exports to non-EU countries. However, growth of EU imports from Mercosur was only about two-thirds of total extra-European import growth (see Table 7.2).

Unfortunately for Mercosur, EU import growth has been rather slow at only 3.7 percent annually in the same time period, compared with 3.4 percent from all of Latin America and 17.4 percent from China. And again, using the entire extra-EU imports as a yardstick, those grew 5.6 percent per year in that period. The definitive issue of interest to Mercosur with regard to the outcome of the expected negotiations is therefore easy to formulate: When, how, and in what sectors can export performance to the EU be improved? The EU will have to use its increasing investment in the Mercosur countries to ensure that those financial flows, combined with technological cooperation, will enable Mercosur to increase its exports to the EU. The list of sensitive goods, to be established during the negotiations, will have to reflect this overriding interest from the Mercosur side.

With regard to investment patterns, the Europeans will have to look at more innovative ways to use their foreign direct investment in Mercosur beyond restricting it mainly to the automobile and pharmaceutical sector, as well as more recently to the services sector, particularly banking (see Tables 7.3 and 7.4 for figures on foreign direct investment). Given the imperative of creating an integrated infrastructure in and among the Mercosur countries, European experience could become a showcase of technological know-how if the necessary financing were to go into long-term direct foreign investment,[5] an area in which the European Investment Bank will certainly be of considerable help. Another interest of the Mercosur countries is the need to attract more foreign investment in the field of small and medium-size enterprises, given that they have the greatest impact on employment. Here again, the strength of the EU economic model is an important point of comparison in biregional relations.

Table 7.1 EU Exports to Mercosur and Selected Regions, 1990–1997 (millions of U.S. dollars unless otherwise noted)

	1990	1991	1992	1993	1994	1995	1996	1997	Average Annual Growth (%)
Mercosur	7,279	8,107	9,468	11,771	15,931	22,221	23,117	25,600	19.7
Latin America	21,736	23,805	28,091	29,702	35,649	42,391	44,525	49,506	12.5
Andean Community	4,522	4,956	5,905	5,480	5,862	7,142	6,926	7,500	7.5
CACM[a]	848	866	1,032	1,155	1,209	1,470	1,385	1,526	8.8
Mexico	5,284	6,401	7,751	7,190	8,247	5,749	6,417	8,100	6.3
United States	104,428	94,847	103,433	106,060	122,436	135,214	144,942	157,300	6.0
Japan	30,911	29,464	28,723	28,790	34,465	43,040	44,978	40,400	3.9
Canada	13,213	12,548	11,970	10,986	12,415	13,586	13,494	15,800	2.6
China	7,373	7,719	9,604	14,301	16,246	19,237	18,407	18,600	14.1
India	8,149	6,826	6,983	7,575	8,679	12,358	12,569	11,700	5.3
ASEAN[b]	22,170	23,183	26,856	30,294	36,438	47,652	51,507	51,000	12.6
CEEC[c]	34,268	35,343	42,426	45,216	56,607	75,489	86,882	97,000	16.0
Mediterranean-II[d]	60,309	58,803	60,816	64,139	66,901	83,026	88,107	61,800	0.3
ACP[e]	21,580	20,122	22,436	19,502	17,240	22,294	22,664	19,570	-1.4
Extra-EU	507,100	494,100	524,900	553,500	627,600	759,200	792,500	854,400	7.7

Source: Direction of Trade Statistics Yearbook 1997 (Washington, D.C.: International Monetary Fund, 1997); *Direction of Trade Statistics Quarterly* (Washington, D.C.: International Monetary Fund, 1998); and estimations and calculations of the Instituto de Relaciones Europeo-Latinoamericanas.

a. CACM (Central American Common Market): Costa Rica, El Salvador, Guatemala, Honduras, and Nicaragua.

b. ASEAN (Association of Southeast Asian Nations): Brunei Darussalam, Indonesia, Malaysia, Philippines, Singapore, Thailand, and Vietnam.

c. CEEC (Central and East European Countries): Albania, Bosnia-Hercegovina, Bulgaria, Czech Republic, Estonia, Croatia, Hungary, Latvia, Lithuania, Macedonia, Poland, Romania, Slovenia, Slovakia, and Yugoslavia (Serbia and Montenegro).

d. Mediterranean-II: twenty Mediterranean Basin countries, excluding the EU.

e. ACP (Africa, the Caribbean, and the Pacific): seventy African, Caribbean, and Pacific countries that are signatories of the Lomé convention.

Table 7.2   EU Imports from Mercosur and Selected Regions, 1990–1997 (millions of U.S. dollars unless otherwise noted)

	1990	1991	1992	1993	1994	1995	1996	1997	Average Annual Growth (%)
Mercosur	17,934	18,697	17,444	15,365	18,527	20,024	19,143	23,200	3.7
Latin America	34,135	34,533	33,166	28,574	34,214	39,841	38,372	43,218	3.4
Andean Community	6,135	6,065	6,089	5,246	6,425	7,609	7,448	7,800	3.5
CACM[a]	1,404	1,442	1,396	1,382	2,070	2,355	2,371	2,466	8.4
Mexico	3,875	3,776	3,799	2,934	3,147	4,059	3,915	4,200	1.2
United States	113,281	120,128	119,882	109,872	122,999	142,175	152,160	170,100	6.0
Japan	67,506	72,063	74,936	66,564	68,982	76,908	72,022	77,700	2.0
Canada	13,130	12,559	12,174	10,072	11,831	15,345	14,539	15,000	1.9
China	13,289	18,160	20,995	23,730	27,644	32,333	34,608	40,900	17.4
India	6,129	6,185	6,573	7,344	8,628	10,434	11,119	11,100	8.9
ASEAN[b]	23,471	27,382	30,836	33,582	39,036	46,466	53,028	58,300	13.9
CEEC[c]	31,251	33,571	38,536	35,639	46,453	61,274	64,453	69,600	12.1
Mediterranean-II[d]	56,439	55,765	55,219	47,297	52,024	59,978	63,074	65,590	2.2
ACP[e]	25,904	24,559	23,744	17,859	22,453	25,396	27,172	24,954	-0.5
Extra-EU	566,500	587,500	596,400	562,800	631,500	745,300	770,600	830,900	5.6

Source: Direction of Trade Statistics Yearbook 1997 (Washington, D.C.: International Monetary Fund, 1997); Direction of Trade Statistics Quarterly (Washington, D.C.: International Monetary Fund, 1998); and estimations and calculations of the Instituto de Relaciones Europeo-Latinoamericanas.

a. CACM (Central American Common Market): Costa Rica, El Salvador, Guatemala, Honduras, and Nicaragua.

b. ASEAN (Association of Southeast Asian Nations): Brunei Darussalam, Indonesia, Malaysia, Philippines, Singapore, Thailand, and Vietnam.

c. CEEC (Central and East European Countries): Albania, Bosnia-Hercegovina, Bulgaria, Czech Republic, Estonia, Croatia, Hungary, Latvia, Lithuania, Macedonia, Poland, Romania, Slovenia, Slovakia, and Yugoslavia (Serbia and Montenegro).

d. Mediterranean-II: twenty Mediterranean Basin countries, excluding the EU.

e. ACP (Africa, the Caribbean, and the Pacific): seventy African, Caribbean, and Pacific countries that are signatories of the Lomé convention.

Table 7.3   Net Foreign Direct Investment Flows to Mercosur, by Main Investor, 1990–1996 (millions of U.S. dollars)

	1990	1991	1992	1993	1994	1995	1996	Average Annual Growth Rate (%), 1990–1996
European Union	928	873	1,136	650	2,324	3,126	4,703	31
United States	1,218	1,284	2,695	4,369	4,484	7,253	3,550	20
Japan	158	366	97	118	33	296	673	27
Total	2,304	2,523	3,928	5,137	6,841	10,675	8,926	25

Source: Foreign Direct Investment in Latin America (Madrid: Inter-American Development Bank and Instituto de Relaciones Europeo-Latinoamericanas, 1998).

Table 7.4   Distribution of Major Flows of Net Foreign Direct Investment to Mercosur, 1990–1996 (percent, unless otherwise noted)

	1990	1991	1992	1993	1994	1995	1996	Average (1990–1996)
European Union	40.3	34.6	28.9	12.7	34.0	29.3	52.7	34.1
Austria	0.0	0.0	0.1	0.1	0.3	0.2	0.1	0.1
Belgium	1.5	−1.1	0.7	−1.3	−1.2	−0.1	5.1	0.8
Denmark	0.0	0.1	0.0	0.0	0.1	0.1	0.3	0.1
Finland	0.7	1.1	0.4	0.2	0.0	0.1	0.0	0.2
France	7.1	−1.7	1.9	2.9	5.1	−1.7	16.4	4.9
Germany	4.9	16.0	2.7	−1.4	8.7	14.1	−1.1	6.3
Italy	2.0	3.6	0.4	−1.2	−0.6	1.0	1.7	0.8
Netherlands	1.9	6.3	11.1	8.6	11.5	1.8	3.9	6.0
Portugal	0.3	0.0	0.1	0.0	0.0	0.3	3.5	0.9
Spain	4.4	2.9	2.9	0.6	1.6	5.9	7.6	4.3
Sweden	0.2	0.2	0.6	0.2	0.2	−0.2	1.6	0.4
United Kingdom	17.3	7.3	7.9	4.0	8.3	7.7	13.8	9.2
United States	52.9	50.9	68.6	85.0	65.5	67.9	39.8	61.6
Japan	6.9	14.5	2.5	2.3	0.5	2.8	7.5	4.3

Source: Foreign Direct Investment in Latin America (Madrid: Inter-American Development Bank and Instituto de Relaciones Europeo-Latinoamericanas, 1998).

There are other shared interests for both partners outside the strictly economic area: Obviously the EU believes in fostering the integration processes in other parts of the world and is willing to provide the necessary know-how from its own process of trial and error over more than forty years. Such know-how can assist Mercosur, even if not all of it will be useful or necessary to the specific integration process of the Southern Cone countries. Already since 1992, in the context of the first interinstitutional agreement between the EC and Mercosur, integration know-how has been transferred, principally in the area of customs regulations and norms and standards, and lately the transfer has expanded into many other fields. One more surprising development could be the introduction of a common currency, which has been under discussion, with a possible starting-date of 2002, where the very recent EU experience could certainly be of some guidance. The euro will not only serve as a possible example for a common currency but also will have some impact on the Mercosur currency transactions, as the duplication of euro-bonds in Brazil and Argentina has demonstrated already in the last two years; as trade grows, it will most likely be dealt with in euros rather than dollars from 1999 onward.

The list of common interests of both partners can be extended in many ways, but serious differences in interests should not be overlooked. These have to do in part with the North-South nature of relations, as they have been characterized in recent years. The Mercosur countries want to achieve not only a more balanced trade relationship but also partnership in a more balanced political relationship, and that relationship can be achieved only if coordinated policies on the international level, be it in the World Trade Organization or the United Nations, become possible. And such policy coordination and interest harmonization between two structurally very different partners might not come without a heavy political price, either one that is paid by the EU itself or by other partners in the international system.

THE PROCESS OF COOPERATION AND NEGOTIATION

The cooperation process with Mercosur has been evolving in the context of EU–Latin American relations, which found their most precise expression in the signing of bilateral third-generation agreements with the EU by all Mercosur members. The next step in reaching out to Mercosur was the interinstitutional agreement, signed on May 29, 1992, between the European Commission and the Common Market Group. That agreement was intended principally as a vehicle for technical assistance, personnel training, and institutional support for the integration process of the then recently founded Mercosur.

The agreement, which now covers cooperation and future negotiations between Mercosur and the EU, is the Interregional Framework Agreement of December 15, 1995, which was signed by all four presidents of Mercosur and their European counterparts in Madrid.[6] It is the first agreement of its type that the EU has concluded outside Europe and is meant to facilitate further negotiations on commercial and economic cooperation while putting in place immediately a political dialogue between the two regions; especially stressed is cooperation in all issues related to regional integration as well as cooperation in wider policy issues such as the environment, the fight against drugs, and the development of new technologies.

This framework agreement could be considered the first phase in the preparation of an association of political as well as economic character. The second phase will be an association agreement, to be signed most likely in 2001, when Mercosur becomes a fully implemented common market. And the third phase would be a free trade association to enter into operation in 2006, at the same time as, according to schedule, the internal transition for some Mercosur sectors comes to an end and hemispheric negotiations on the FTAA process might be concluded. In the EU, if all goes well, the reform of the European Union's Common Agricultural Policy will be in place. Furthermore, it is by no means a coincidence that this is the same time horizon envisaged by the EU for incorporation of the first wave of new members from Eastern Europe—this schedule would guarantee the Mercosur countries that their market access conditions were equal to those of the Eastern European countries then joining the EU. There has been concern on the Latin American side that there might be considerable competition in some sectors between Eastern European countries and the Mercosur countries with regard to the EU market, especially in the agriculture sector, which accounts for more than 40 percent of Mercosur's exports to the EU.[7] Therefore, the negotiating pressure from Mercosur will be geared toward ensuring that its members are treated the same as their competitors in Eastern Europe and at a similar pace.

Given the impressive adherence of Mercosur to its program, established since the signing of the Treaty of Asunción, and the similar fulfillment of the European Union's schedules with regard to the single market and the European Monetary Union, there can be little doubt about the political commitment of both sides to stick to such an agenda. That does not mean that the road will be an easy one, given that the stakes are high and that there will be countervailing interests within and outside both integration mechanisms, which will try to influence the agenda to their own benefit.

What were the immediate steps taken and on what levels are cooperation and negotiation currently pursued? It is typical of the European Union that there exists a complicated, but necessary, legal mechanism for the implementation of the framework agreement. Those legal requirements are especially difficult for the negotiation process, since the framework agreement is of a mixed character, meaning that it will be negotiated in parallel by the European Commission (covering its competencies: trade and cooperation) and by the member states (for their competencies: investments and services). Such a negotiating mechanism is meant to ensure that the agreement can go forward toward a reciprocal and progressive liberalization in all fields of trade and trade-related measures. So far, only 14 percent of EU-Mercosur trade has been considered to be in sensitive products.

Although the commission does not yet have a formal negotiating mandate from the European Council, each side has established a "photograph" of all trade and service-related activities to find common ground for the negotiations. In that context, it is no accident that the European office of Eurostat has been giving technical assistance to the Mercosur countries to bring their statistical apparatus up to the level needed to enable easy comparisons with the EU.

This photograph on the European side consists of a series of comparative analyses of distinct aspects in commercial relations between the regions from 1990 to 1996. It analyzed not only product trade but also the trade in services and the regulation of such services in Mercosur. Special attention was given to the photograph of norms and commercial disciplines, such as sanitary and phytosanitary regulations, rules of origins, rules of competition, and instruments of commercial defense. As might be expected, comparisons of the regulatory framework and the instruments used by each side to defend its commercial interests have demonstrated notable differences, and only when those differences are taken into account can the upcoming negotiations develop in a meaningful way.

When the formal negotiations will start and how long those negotiations will take is an open question, but, for political reasons, both the EU and Mercosur would like to demonstrate advances at the upcoming first EU–Latin American summit of presidents and heads of government in the first semester of 1999 in Rio, where Mercosur will be the center of attention, given that from a European viewpoint relations with those countries are a priority within the overall context of EU–Latin American relations. The interregional cooperation framework agreement establishes cooperation on two levels: (1) the political dialogue that includes regular meetings at presidential, ministerial, and technical levels as well as a parliamentary dimension between the European Parliament and the Parliamentary Commission of the Mercosur countries, and (2) the Cooperation Council, which consists of the European Council plus the European Commission and the Mercosur Council plus the member states. The Cooperation Council created a joint committee, which supervises a subcommittee on trade.

The subcommittee on trade met for the first time on November 5–6, 1996, in Belo Horizonte. There it was decided to establish three working groups on access to the product market, access to the services market, and the question of trade norms and disciplines, reflecting very much the discussions that were taking place on both sides to establish the photograph of economic relations between Mercosur and the EU. The third meeting of the subcommittee, on November 29, 1997, in Punta del Este, finalized the photograph. The final meeting of the subcommittee, on May 14, 1998, in Brussels, gave a green light to the preparation of a joint document, which will serve as a basis for the negotiating mandate.

Cooperation between the two integration mechanisms also obviously has its financial side, given that the EU and its member states are the principal donors to the Mercosur countries, accounting for 67.2 percent of all aid received in 1996 (the second donor was Japan, accounting for about 30.7 percent). The principal bilateral European donors to Mercosur have been Germany, Italy, and Spain. The European Commission alone supplied, between 1990 and 1997, 488 million ECUs to Mercosur and its member states. Economic cooperation programs, in particular, are likely to increase, inasmuch as the Mercosur countries will find it necessary during the negotiations to ask for specific cooperation programs from the European side to facilitate preparations for a more liberal trade arrangement with the EU.

THE COSTS AND BENEFITS OF INTERREGIONAL ASSOCIATION

An interregional association can be considered a "new animal" in the international system because, as demonstrated here, it goes far beyond a free trade area and has effects in a great number of fields for both integration mechanisms and their member states. Both sides will, therefore, have to calculate very carefully the costs and benefits of such an "association," which seems to have become the key word of a new type of alliance, a more politically correct expression for joining forces in a global marketplace.[8] Such costs and benefits are difficult to calculate and obviously change over time, inasmuch as the international environment changes (economically and otherwise). Internal agreement within each bloc cannot be achieved easily, since some member states on each side see such a development as dangerous for specific sectors of their economies and especially with regard to more traditional alliances, questioning the compatibility of the new arrangement with the existing strong relations that each bloc has with the United States. This matter becomes even more complicated, because each bloc has a distinct external agenda and both blocs face the issue of widening and deepening, an issue that is not easily reconciled either in the EU or in Mercosur.

Given that integration is a dynamic process that creates its own "push and pull" factors in each geographic environment, the attractiveness of successful integration processes (and both blocs can count themselves in that group) makes widening almost a geopolitical and geoeconomic necessity. But that frequently means the loss of markets and loss of influence for third actors, who then want to be "compensated" by the integration group for those losses. Such discussions between the EU—after the widening processes of the European Union—and the United States go back a long way, and similar problems are likely to arise for Mercosur in the event of the consolidation of a South American Free Trade Area (SAFTA) in 2000, which would then grant its members better access to Mercosur than the United States would enjoy.

It is in this context that the ongoing discussions about the creation of an FTAA have to be seen. It is by no means certain to what extent it would be possible for Mercosur to have parallel negotiations for an EU-Mercosur free trade agreement (FTA) and an FTAA with the entire hemisphere, given that the United States obviously wants to ensure that it will not be marginalized in a market with the importance of Mercosur. Inasmuch as the EU assumes the same strategy, one has only to consider topics such as norms and standards to see that the possibility of "having your cake and eating it"—giving preferences and similar access to both of the principal outside traders and investors—will be a very difficult goal to achieve.

The other danger of an interregional association is that it might become no more than a negotiating asset of Mercosur for achieving a better result within the Americas. Here the negotiating capacity of the Mercosur countries will have to weather a severe test in the years to come, but at the same time, given the competition between the EU and the United States to forge stronger links with Mercosur, it will gain quite a bit of international status and prominence. EU enlargement and its future relations with the Mediterranean countries have created certain doubts on Mercosur's part about the reliability of the EU's interest in Mercosur. Statistics might help explain. Eastern Europe and the Mediterranean together do not constitute an emerging market of similar importance to Mercosur, not least because of the population and the industrial capacity involved. But seen strictly from the viewpoint of the EU, opportunities and challenges presented by proximity have a profound impact on policymaking and on policy priorities, even on economic policy choices, as the case of NAFTA has demonstrated so clearly for the United States.

In spite of all the real and possible costs of an interregional association between the EU and Mercosur, there are a number of obvious benefits for both sides: One can start with a new role for central integration powers, meaning that Brazil and Germany assume a new function within integrated regional blocs, where their policies are more geared toward achieving consensus and harmonization of interests with their neighbors than toward exercising traditional regional leadership. In this context, it should be stressed that Brazil and Germany are already the strongest bilateral partners within EU-Mercosur relations.

Another obvious point is that the increase of bargaining power in the international system will strengthen both regions. Mercosur will feel the effect more strongly, given the current asymmetry of power between the

EU and Mercosur, but even for the EU the effect of such an important alliance partner should not be underestimated. And from this increased bargaining power should result a stronger voice in the international system when the new rules of the international marketplace are formulated. The EU, like Mercosur, has independently complained at various times about the unilateral position of the United States and its capacity to gain the upper hand in many international negotiations. Given a free trade area of 700 million consumers in 2006 between the expanded EU and an expanded Mercosur such a situation could very easily be redressed.

Looking more toward relations between the two blocs and not so much at their place among other international players, increased trade and investment between them would create more competitiveness and better prepare them for the challenges of globalization. In that context, it should also not be underestimated that development within each region will be affected by the development of relations between them, as an indicator of increasing interdependence. This new relationship will be built on the concept of mutual benefit, and it is very likely to produce just that.

To maintain an internal consensus on both sides about the long-term usefulness of such an association will probably be the most difficult task, since the weakest member in each group might try to minimize the cost of such a new alliance in favor of short-term gains for its own country.[9] Several types of scenarios can be envisaged in this regard. The maturity of policymaking can be demonstrated only after the negotiations between the two sides have been concluded without each side claiming a better representation of their national or regional interests. Only then will it be possible to talk about a new alliance.

NOTES

1. The EU has a political dialogue in place with over one hundred countries either directly or with a group of countries. The latter form is certainly preferred. See Enrique González Sánchez, "El diálogo político de la Unión Europea con países terceros," *Revista de Derecho Comunitario Europeo* 1 (January–June 1997): 79.

2. See Alfredo Picerno and Pablo Gutiérrez, "Notas sobre la convergencia entre el Mercosur y la Unión Europea," working paper series 77, Centro Latinoamericano de Economía Humana, Montevideo, Uruguay, 1997, p. 54.

3. See Inter-American Development Bank [IDB] and Instituto de Relaciones Europeo-Latinoamericanas [IRELA], *Foreign Direct Investment in Latin America* (Madrid: IDB and IRELA, 1998).

4. Quote from Francisco Bataller M., "The Relations Between the European Union and Mercosur: Policies, Achievements and Prospects," *EU/LDC News* 3 (December 1996): 2.

5. See Héctor N. Di Biase, "Acuerdo Mercosur–Unión Europea: El paso a la segunda fase," *Cuaderno de Negocios Internacionales e Integración* (November–December 1996) (Universidad Católica, Montevideo, Uruguay), p. 39.

6. For the text and all related EU-Mercosur documents, see Roberto Dromi and Carlos Molina del Pozo, *Acuerdo Mercosur Unión Europea* (Madrid: Ediciones Ciudad Argentina, 1996).

7. For an evaluation of the possible competition between Eastern Europe and Latin America for the EU market, see Instituto de Relaciones Europeo-Latinoamericanas [IRELA], *Closer EU Links with Eastern Europe: Implications for Latin America* (Madrid: IRELA, 1997).

8. For an early treatment of the possible EU-Mercosur alliance, see Félix Peña, "El Mercosur y la Unión Europea: El Camino hacia una Nueva Alianza Interregional," *Anuario de las Relaciones Europeo-Latinoamericanas* (1993) (Instituto de Relaciones Europeo-Latinoamericanas, Madrid), pp. 133–155.

9. For a preliminary analysis of the benefits and obstacles of the association, see "Preparing the EU-Mercosur Association," an IRELA briefing (1998) (Madrid, Instituto de Relaciones Europeo-Latinoamericanas).

8

U.S. Policy Toward Mercosur: From Miami to Santiago

Riordan Roett

In less than four years, the debate regarding economic integration in the Americas dramatically changed. The goal of the U.S. government in Miami in December 1994—to create a Free Trade Area of the Americas (FTAA) by the year 2005—was thwarted by both U.S. domestic politics and developments in the Western Hemisphere. The second Summit of the Americas in Santiago, Chile, in 1998 proved uneventful, given the absence of fast-track negotiating authority for President Bill Clinton. And the continued maturing of Mercosur strengthened the resolve of the Mercosur countries, in particular Brazil, to retain as much autonomy as possible to further strengthen the common market before entering into more ample negotiations for an FTAA.

The prognosis for the remainder of the Clinton administration, with regard to hemispheric integration, is low-key activity driven by U.S. domestic political considerations, absent the enthusiasm and drive that was evident in Miami. This will leave Mercosur a great deal of room to maneuver in designing the negotiations process in the next century, pursuing a deeper relationship with the European Union (EU), and deciding on the appropriate balance between broadening and deepening. In these debates, the United States will have a relatively minor voice.

THE UNITED STATES AND WESTERN HEMISPHERE INTEGRATION

In this chapter I address three issues that shape U.S. policy toward hemispheric integration. The first consideration in analyzing the U.S. response to Mercosur is the complicated and often complex bilateral relationship with Brazil. Although rarely stated openly, there has been deep skepticism in official Washington, D.C., for many years about Brazil's role in the

Americas. The perceived pompousness of Itamarati, the Brazilian foreign ministry, which is charged with responsibility for trade negotiations as well as traditional diplomatic tasks, was tolerable so long as Brazil—and the rest of the Southern Cone—appeared toothless and generally accepted U.S. leadership. When the creation of Mercosur provided Brazil and its neighbors with a new and dynamic platform to offer an alternative vision of the future of South America, the U.S. policy community gave it little importance. The general attitude was that this initiative, like many others before it, would collapse because Brazil could not cure its assorted deficits. The poor record of regional collaboration, when seen against a background of 150 years of subregional rivalries and competition, strengthened the impression that little of substance would emerge from subregional talks.

A second consideration is the U.S. experience with the North American Free Trade Agreement (NAFTA). The lengthy preparations for the Miami Summit in December 1994—in which Brazil was regarded as a spoiler by the United States—were undertaken in the afterglow of the perceived success of NAFTA. Begun under the Bush administration, and successfully approved by Congress during the first Clinton administration, the three-nation agreement became a White House mantra for a new relationship with Latin America. On the success of NAFTA would a broad, encompassing free trade of the Americas arrangement be constructed. The success of NAFTA was linked to the growing rapprochement between the United States and Mexico, a result of the apparently spectacular economic success of the presidency of Carlos Salinas de Gortari (1988–1994).

The boom in trade and investment and the enthusiasm in Washington and Mexico City over the maturing of the bilateral relationship fostered the perception in the United States that NAFTA would be the foundation of a historic effort to create a Free Trade Area of the Americas. Unknown to either Washington or Mexico City, however, the enthusiasm for broader integration efforts was to be dealt a lethal blow with the devaluation of the Mexican peso a few weeks after the conclusion of the Miami Summit.

The peso devaluation and the dramatic shift in trade relations between the two countries placed the U.S. administration in an untenable position. When it sought to construct a safety net for Mexico, it encountered a firestorm in the Congress. Criticism of the so-called bailout came from both the left—U.S. workers would lose jobs with the loss of the export market in Mexico—and the right—bailouts were antimarket and those involved should shoulder the financial losses. The administration abandoned early efforts to involve Congress in the rescue of the Mexican economy and acted unilaterally.

That decision—whether correct or not—highlights the third factor that strongly affects the U.S. position regarding new trade initiatives in the Americas: domestic politics. Mindful of the dramatic fallout from the

Mexican peso devaluation and the loud public response, the White House decided in late 1997 to postpone a request for congressional approval of fast-track negotiating authority, which would have permitted the president to proceed with the ambitious program outlined in Miami. The political dynamic in Washington in 1995 and 1996 left the administration ambiguous about its goals for integration. Although the mantra indicated that the second summit would establish a clear process for negotiations, without fast-track legislation it was difficult to imagine a very dynamic follow-up to Miami. And by 1995 and 1996 it was clear that the Brazilian Plano Real was working, that Brazil and Mercosur were in a process of broadening (Bolivia and Chile joined as associate members), and that Chile had abandoned any hope of becoming the fourth "amigo" of NAFTA, as had been planned in Miami.

The White House, yielding to world events, took the decision in early 1998 to sacrifice fast track for the International Monetary Fund (IMF). In the president's State of the Union message on January 27, he paid lip service to the fast-track concept but clearly emphasized the greater priority of congressional support for funding for the IMF, given the growing turmoil in Asian financial markets. As the *New York Times* reported, "Mr. Clinton's top economic and foreign policy aides concluded it would be all but impossible to get Congressional approval for both the IMF commitments and the trade legislation, which was withdrawn late last year after Mr. Clinton could not overcome resistance in his own party."[1]

The outlook for hemisphere-wide economic integration after the second Summit of the Americas is bleak. The White House will attempt to reassure Latin American participants that it continues to support the general goals of Miami. The president retains the authority to negotiate tariff reductions and minor changes in trade policies and regulations, but comprehensive negotiations, without fast-track authority, are improbable given the uncertainty of ultimate congressional approval. The debate about new initiatives for the Americas must now await the outcome of the U.S. presidential election in 2000.

The United States and Brazil

Relations between the United States and the dominant partner in Mercosur have gone through kaleidoscopic changes over the decades. A "special relationship" existed early in the century, in which Brazil sought U.S. support, in large part to counterbalance a more powerful and often menacing Argentina. That link yielded in the 1950s and 1960s to tensions created by Brazilian nationalism. There was a brief honeymoon after the overthrow of the Goulart government in 1964, but it quickly yielded to a new sense of Brazilian exceptionalism in its trade and foreign policies. Relations were exacerbated in the Ford and Carter administrations over diverse issues such as nuclear fuel rods and human rights. With the transition in Brazil—and in much of South America—from authoritarian to democratic governments in the 1980s, relations turned pragmatic. In a sharp turnabout, Argentina in the 1990s identified its foreign policy increasingly with the United States, whereas Brazil struck out on its own and reasserted that it was primus inter pares in South America. For the first time since independence from Spain, that position was generally accepted by Brazil's Spanish-American neighbors. Brazil let it be known that it sought a more independent posture with regard to Washington that would best serve its—and by extension, the continent's—interests.

The Brazilian position was driven by the sophisticated, if inbred, foreign ministry, Itamarati. Occupying a particularly strong position in both the formulation and implementation of policy, the ministry gained new significance as it emerged as Brazil's key trade negotiator, particularly in multilateral forums. What held Itamarati back was the long-standing fragility of the Brazilian economy, which undercut diplomatic efforts to seek a weightier role for Brazil in international and hemispheric affairs. With the implementation of the Plano Real in 1994 and the expansion of Mercosur, Brazilian diplomacy gained a new dynamism. Inevitably, the assertion of Brazilian regional leadership would be viewed in Washington as less than helpful in implementing U.S. policy goals. The cordiality of relations among the NAFTA partners—Canada, Mexico, and the United States—was seen in Washington as a natural consequence of the deepening economic relationship among them. Would Brazil accept NAFTA as the logical building block for hemispheric integration or seek to impose its own vision?

In preparations for the Miami Summit, Brazil was characterized by the United States as a difficult interlocutor. On the long road to Miami, a number of proposals were drafted and circulated. One had been prepared by the Rio Group, in which Brazil was an active member.[2] The Rio Group draft document was submitted to the United States a week before one of the final preparatory meetings. "Short on specific action items, firm commitments, and accountable mechanisms for implementation," another report read, "the Rio Group draft presented precisely the outcome the United States had been working to circumvent and that cascading modular multilateralism intended to surpass."[3] As the Brazilian delegation, led by Itamarati vice minister Roberto Abdenur, arrived at the conference center outside Washington, D.C., the U.S. delegation "was offended by Abdenur's preachy, paternalistic presentation, even as it respected America's chief interlocutor with the conference hosts."[4] The next morning, in a meeting of the Rio Group with a ranking U.S. official, "the Brazilians sought to stir up latent resentments against the United States, to foster fears that Washington would use the summit agreements to monitor their activities and intervene in their domestic affairs."[5] And in a midnight drafting session the Brazilians dwelled on the nuances of each word, working hard to twist the Plan of Action in the direction of the Itamarati world view.

The following morning, Abdenur told the other Rio Group countries that the United States was showing respect for the Rio Group text—taking a constructive attitude, and the Latin Americans could respond in kind. As the instigator of conflict, and having attained the respect and leadership role they had sought with such tenacity, the Brazilian diplomats could now play peacemaker.[6]

Whether or not the Brazilian delegation's performance was as contentious as claimed, the Clinton administration often finds it difficult to understand that a new dynamic has emerged in the hemisphere following the "lost decade" of the 1980s and the initiation of liberalization and market reforms in the 1990s. All of the states in the southern part of the South American continent have a renewed interest in and commitment to subregional integration. The goal of economic integration has a number of components. Trade and services are important, of course, but the creation of Mercosur implies certain broad political and foreign policy goals for the participating nations, especially Brazil. This is usually overlooked or thought to be irrelevant or transitory by the United States.

The United States and Mercosur

The United States has a long record of entering into trade and financial agreements for specific, narrow goals that usually emphasize market access, profit, and an expanded role for the private sector. Mercosur, closer in design and intent to the European Union, is intrinsically linked to the restoration of civilian government in the region in the 1980s. It is viewed as an important step in the consolidation of democracy. Mercosur is also viewed as a historical turning point in the long-standing animosities that characterized the region for decades. The common market concept is meant to offer an opportunity to pursue valued goals of social and physical integration. Over time, Mercosur is expected to develop a modest set of institutions to deal with imperatives such as dispute resolution and regulatory requirements. But in the long run, the expectation is that Mercosur will consider basic steps toward supranationalism. Although no timetable is in place, and there is no hurry to set one, the deepening of the arrangement in the future is seen as both logical and desirable.

In contrast, NAFTA is a trade arrangement, pure and simple. There is no thought of supranationalism, nor is there any tradition in U.S. diplomacy to seek the sort of political arrangements that are emerging within Mercosur. The summits of the Mercosur presidents have become the principal mechanism for joint decisionmaking. These meetings are buttressed by the active role of the Rio Group, the Ibero-American summits, and other regional and subregional arrangements that are embedded in the political processes of the countries involved and increasingly have an impact on their foreign policies.[7] The scheduled summit with the EU in 1999 may have greater importance than the Americas summits for South America, because there are more similarities between the EU and Mercosur than between NAFTA and Mercosur.[8] The EU-Mercosur agenda is more nuanced diplomatically and politically than the narrower, trade-focused relationship between the United States and Mercosur.

The difficulty the United States has in giving Mercosur the importance it deserves was captured in the January 1997 congressional hearing to confirm Charlene Barshefsky as U.S. Trade Representative (USTR). Testifying before the U.S. Senate Finance Committee, Barshefsky was asked about the absence of fast-track authority and whether or not the United States was "causing us to lose out in South America." She replied, "I think the absence of fast track leaves a vacuum in our own hemisphere with respect to leadership and with respect to the rules of trade in our hemisphere. What the absence has done has been to lead to an agglomeration by other countries of other trading partners in our own hemisphere as a means of building their own little unit or system of rules and obligations. Mercosur is one such example."[9]

Barshefsky's comments were not well received in Mercosur, of course, but, again, they indicate the difficulty that policymakers in Washington have in taking seriously those regional initiatives that are not directly responsive to U.S. policy interests. This was illustrated in the comments of a former U.S. policymaker remarking on Brazil's role in Miami at the Summit of the Americas:

> The heart of the drama of Miami was Brazil's struggle to establish itself as the interlocutor for South America and the Rio Group. . . . Itamarati has already accomplished its main strategic objective of consolidating Mercosur and pulling other South American countries into the Mercosur orbit through a series of bilateral and subregional trade agreements, thereby establishing Brazil as the logical lead South American representative in any negotiations with the United States and its NAFTA partners on the terms of hemispheric trade integration.[10]

The insinuation is clear—Brazil is deliberately and mischievously opposing U.S. initiatives and leadership. The implication also is that Brazil is not entitled (or prepared) to exercise regional leadership, a role that is generally acknowledged by its neighbors and now partners in the Mercosur integration effort to exist de facto.

The frustration in Washington over Brazil's initiatives continued after the Miami Summit during a series of ministerial and vice-ministerial meetings convened to follow up on the Miami agenda and prepare for the 1998 summit in Santiago. In perhaps the most important of these encounters, in

Belo Horizonte, Brazil, in May 1997, the United States formally acknowledged that the FTAA should coexist with subregional trade groups such as NAFTA—and Mercosur. This was an important concession by the United States. The Argentine foreign minister, Guido di Tella, commented after the Belo Horizonte meeting that "we think the Americans have at last recognized that the sub-regional groups are beneficial—while we have convinced them of our keenness to go ahead with an FTAA."[11]

But Brazil, again, was seen as an adversary of the United States when, at the Belo Horizonte session, Brazilian foreign minister Luiz Felipe Lampreia commented that "no sane country would negotiate twice" over tariff reductions. President Fernando Henrique Cardoso reemphasized that point when he echoed his foreign minister, stating that "as long as President Clinton does not have authorization from Congress, the talks are imaginary."[12]

As President Cardoso indicated, without fast-track authority the U.S. delegations at these meetings were able to do little but reiterate and support the rhetoric of the Miami Summit and hold out the hope that Congress would endorse fast track. By 1997 and 1998, that rhetoric was outdated. Increasingly, Mercosur was viewed as viable not so much as an alternative to the FTAA but as an important, autonomous entity that at some point would determine an appropriate policy response to the FTAA.

The wariness in the U.S.-Brazil relationship is long standing and will be a constant in hemispheric affairs for the foreseeable future. The United States will continue to believe that its initial idea of an FTAA should—and will—dominate trade arrangements in the hemisphere. Brazil will continue to believe that its commitment to subregional integration is logical and best serves the interests of Brazilian foreign policy. Although these differences will not seriously damage relations between the two states, the misunderstandings will be perpetuated by the bureaucracies in both countries, which react to stereotypes and perceptions. Although personal relations between the two chief executives are cordial, day-to-day policy initiatives are taken principally by Itamarati in Brazil and by the State Department, National Security Council, and office of the USTR in the United States. At that level, both sides will continue to see competition rather than collaboration as the modus operandi for hemisphere-wide trade negotiations.

THE UNITED STATES AND REGIONAL INTEGRATION
AFTER THE MEXICAN PESO DEVALUATION

Although there had been significant domestic opposition to NAFTA during the original negotiations, the final vote in the U.S. Congress, when combined with the apparent economic success of Mexico under Carlos Salinas, muted the naysayers. Evidently, it was quickly forgotten in the White House that the strongest opposition to NAFTA came from within the Democratic Party and the labor unions, longtime supporters of the party. For U.S. policymakers, NAFTA's success was a logical building block on which to extend the free trade concept throughout the Americas. That was the aim of the Miami Summit. The declaration that free trade negotiations in the Americas would be concluded by 2005 was the bedrock of U.S. policy in the hemisphere. But with the spectacular collapse of the Mexican peso in late December 1994, the U.S. administration was put on the defensive with regard to both the rescue package for Mexico in 1995 and plans for immediate expansion of NAFTA, which would serve as the basis for the FTAA.[13]

Commenting on the post-Miami atmosphere in Washington, D.C., one participant stated,

> As it had in 1994, in 1995 the administration again abandoned efforts to gain fast-track approval and NAFTA-parity legislation. Fast-track continued to founder over the inability of Congress and the White House to find common ground on labor rights and environmental protection. The Republicans on the House Ways and Means Committee wanted a clear bill that, while not explicitly excluding labor and the environment from trade agreements, would not require their inclusion, but U.S. Trade Representative (USTR) Mickey Kantor insisted on explicit inclusion.[14]

The case of Chile shows the negative repercussions of the administration's failure to gain fast-track authority. Chile had been promised membership in NAFTA by the Clinton administration and had publicly and enthusiastically accepted the invitation. Following the Mexican devaluation, however, it was thought that any request for fast track would be turned down by the Congress. Plans to expand NAFTA drifted. As one commentator noted, "The Chilean government was furious with the Clinton administration when it abandoned efforts to secure fast-track authority. President Eduardo Frei complained bitterly to visiting Americans, making it clear that having been jilted first by Bush and then by Clinton, the Chileans considered the United States an unreliable ally. Please, no more promises about fast track, the Chileans told visiting U.S. diplomats, just let us know when you have congressional authority in hand."[15]

As the administration agonized over whether or not to request fast track following the Miami Summit, the Chileans took matters into their own hands. The Frei government successfully negotiated associate status with Mercosur and refocused its trade strategy to emphasize bilateral trade arrangements, thereby obviating the need for a NAFTA linkage. The loser has been the United States in terms of trade flows: "Chile, tired of waiting for President Clinton to win renewal of fast-track authority to sign a free trade accord with Santiago, has turned to other trading partners, including Canada and Mexico, and American corporations are losing hundreds of millions of dollars a year."[16] The report continued:

> As Chile has signed free trade agreements with other nations, the increase in imports of U.S. products has slowed from a 43 percent jump in 1995 to almost zero growth in 1997. In part, that is because Chile's accords with Mexico and Canada have made products from those nations more competitive. But it is also because such multinational corporations as Chrysler Corp. and IBM have stopped shipping many products from U.S. factories to Chilean docks, switching instead to products made in their Canadian and Mexican plants to take advantage of lower tariffs.[17]

The loss of Chile as a logical fourth partner in NAFTA, the continuing skepticism in U.S. political and labor circles about the Mexican recovery, and the absence of fast-track authority has produced a stalemate in trade talks between the United States and the rest of the hemisphere. That stalemate appears intractable. The White House is unable to muster sufficient support in the Democratic Party to get a vote in favor of fast track; Republicans are unwilling to shoulder the political burden of giving the Democratic president trade authorization and leaving them open in the upcoming elections to the accusation that they are not sensitive to labor and environmental standards.

U.S. DOMESTIC POLITICS

In a dramatic demonstration that all politics are local, President Clinton was forced to abandon his quest for fast-track authority in November 1997. The decision to walk away was viewed in Washington as the worst defeat for the White House since the withdrawal of the president's proposal for nationwide health care. Although Clinton vowed to renew his request for fast track in 1998, it is now clear that the administration has other priorities. Trade negotiations in the Americas will have little appeal for the remainder of Clinton's second term. What happened?

All presidents since 1974 have been given fast-track authority by the Congress for a specific period of time. Clinton's authorization expired in April 1994. Because of the difficulty in gaining approval of NAFTA, the White House decided to bide its time. Not until the January 1997 State of the Union message did the president call for a renewal of his authority, and not until September 1997 did the White House open the campaign for it. On September 10, the president formally requested the authority in a speech at the White House, but no formal legislation was submitted, given sharp differences of opinion within the administration on the appropriate wording.

For the next two months, fast track was front and center in the partisan and ideological debates in the U.S. Congress. It is now conceded that the White House failed to judge the depth of the opposition to the initiative. First, and most serious, the president found himself in November with strenuous objection to fast track from 80 percent of the Democrats in the House of Representatives. Second, the Republicans, although more sympathetic, were unwilling to rescue a Democratic president if his own party was hostile. Third, the debate about fast track demonstrated the reassertion of political clout by the American Federation of Labor–Congress of Industrial Organizations (AFL-CIO), the grand confederation of labor unions. The combined opposition finally led the president to request that the legislation be withdrawn hours before a vote was scheduled on the House floor.

The Democratic Party has had a prickly relationship with the Clinton White House. Many in the Congress believe that the president has abandoned many of the traditional interests of the party in attempting to carve out a position for himself as a centrist. Much of the blame for the loss of control of the House in the November 1994 elections is attributed to the president and his policies. A very significant element in the party's position was the strong and public opposition to fast track by Congressman Richard Gephardt, leader of the Democratic minority and likely Speaker of the House had the Democrats regained a majority in the 1998 congressional elections. Gephardt aligned himself early in the debate with those demanding environmental and labor standards in any fast-track legislation. It should be noted that Gephardt is the probable challenger to Vice President Al Gore for the Democratic Party presidential nomination in 2000. His stand against fast track will certainly build goodwill among important working-class constituencies across America.

As the debate opened, Gephardt, who had just returned from a visit to South America, stated that he was more convinced than ever that the only acceptable trade accords are those that "place labor rights and environmental protection in the core of every treaty," the same position that the U.S. labor movement was strenuously defending.[18] "Labor rights" were understood to mean, in the code words used in debate in the Congress, a commitment from trading partners to raise workers' wages. For most less-developed nations, those wages are their main comparative advantage—many U.S. firms have relocated overseas precisely because of the wage differential. But for Gephardt and his supporters, the wage issue was of growing concern among organized workers in the United States. It was easily exploitable in constituencies across the country, and workers were a large voting bloc for the Democratic Party.

The environmental concerns espoused by Gephardt and his backers meant that they wanted a commitment to far greater enforcement of environmental laws, to which Mexico had agreed in a side pact with NAFTA. Even the administration concedes that the side agreements have been largely ignored, however, so Gephardt wanted them included in the body of the legislation. Rallying their traditional working-class base of support and adding environmental groups, Gephardt and his allies were able to build a strong argument against the pending legislation.

The White House, on the defensive, tried to pull together an unwieldy coalition of business, Republicans who generally favor free trade but without side agreements, and moderate Democrats. Ironically, Clinton's strongest ally in the House was the Republican Speaker, Newt Gingrich, who favored passage of the legislation, on his party's terms. In the end, the Republican leadership let it be known that they would not support the legislation if the White House failed to deliver the Democratic votes needed for passage or if they equivocated on the labor and environmental issues.

The president and vice president traveled to Capitol Hill in mid-September to rally the Democratic troops, but they ran into strong skepticism from the party caucus. Clinton received the same message at the annual convention of the AFL-CIO in Pittsburgh in September; Gephardt received a standing ovation from the assembly. As the draft legislation moved through committee, a preliminary vote was taken in early October in the House Ways and Means Committee, which has jurisdiction over trade matters. The vote was twenty-four to fourteen in favor of fast track, but only four Democrats on the committee voted with the administration.

In the last few days before a scheduled vote in the House, the fast-track legislation became hostage to one of the most difficult domestic political issues—abortion. The president's efforts to round up sufficient Democratic votes became snared in a highly emotional debate in the House over the financing of family planning programs overseas. Opponents of family planning and abortion wanted the president to rescind U.S. financial support for international organizations that provide or counsel abortions. The president stood to lose votes no matter what he decided. A partisan squabble also broke out over how to conduct the national census in 2000, with some Republicans, generally favorable to fast track, threatening to vote no unless Clinton dropped his plans to use sampling rather than direct counting. Their position was clear—sampling would probably favor Democratic congressional districts.

In the early hours of November 10, the president called the Speaker. The House Republican leadership then announced that they were shelving the fast-track bill at the president's request rather than allow the measure to be defeated. The next day, the president assumed responsibility for the defeat. But the White House repeatedly asked itself why, when the economy was booming and U.S. corporations were globally competitive, did Congress become convinced that trade threatened the livelihoods of working Americans? There is no simple answer. Generally, though, the perception is that although Americans have mostly benefited from the dramatic expansion of world trade, there are losers, and those losers are often concentrated in particular industries and particular congressional districts. They are far more likely to hold union jobs. Workers who have not finished high school are particularly vulnerable to job loss that arises from competition with lower-cost producers abroad. And they vote Democratic in large numbers.

It was also clear, after the defeat, that the administration had failed to take into account the concern over the impact of NAFTA—and the Mexican devaluation—on the U.S. workforce. The White House had wildly oversold the benefits of free trade to ordinary workers in 1993 during the NAFTA debate. Those unfulfilled promises came back to haunt the administration in the final weeks of the fast-track discussion in Congress.

The campaign against fast track demonstrated the renewed power in national politics of organized labor. The AFL-CIO worked closely with Gephardt and the anti–fast-track forces in the House. Union money has grown increasingly important for House Democrats, whose financial support from business began to disappear after the Republicans won control of Congress in 1994. By 1996 contributions from labor's political action committees (PACs) jumped to 48 percent of all PAC donations to House Democrats, up from 33 percent in 1992. Labor unions began mobilizing against fast track early in 1997 and waged an energetic campaign at the grassroots level to pressure members of Congress to vote against fast track. Labor's efforts against the trade bill were joined by environmental groups, consumer safety groups, and civil rights organizations.

In mid-September the AFL-CIO went on the air in twenty key congressional districts with advertisements opposing the measure, and they spent $1.5 to $2.0 million through early November.[19] It was organized labor's biggest showdown with the White House since unions lost their battle in 1993 over NAFTA. Given the concentrated political power of the unions, and the growing dependence of the rank-and-file Democrats on PAC contributions from labor, it was probably inevitable that the White House would fail to win the necessary votes. The dramatic increase in the importance of labor financing for Democratic campaigns suggests that the outlook for fast track in the future is not rosy. There is little reason to believe that the House Democrats and the unions and their allies will find free trade arrangements any more compelling in the future than they did in 1997, given the perceived negative impact of globalization on the U.S. working class.

The Clinton administration now faces the prospect of a final two years in power without fast-track legislation. During the president's whirlwind visit to South America in October 1997, he made free trade the crux of his agenda. He declared a new era of economic partnership with the region, insisting that he would make negotiations for a hemisphere-wide free trading bloc the focus of the second summit in Santiago in 1998. But the political realities in Washington indicate that hemisphere initiatives are on permanent hold and that the fault lines in the Congress will remain deeply entrenched until the next presidential election.

The reaction in Latin America to the White House defeat was immediate. Foreign Minister José Miguel Insulza of Chile commented that "in the eyes of the [Chilean] public, it is another disappointment. Our expectations were much higher. . . . We now see free trade with the U.S. as a more remote possibility."[20] And although perhaps not in direct response to President Clinton's failure to gain fast-track authority, the Andean Pact and Mercosur states announced in November 1997 their plan to form a single free trade area. Foreign ministers at the Ibero-American summit in Venezuela pledged to intensify negotiations to reach an agreement.[21] The nine nations form a market of 310 million consumers with a joint gross domestic product in excess of $1,200 billion. It may well be that the impetus for increased trade integration will follow similar subregional lines for the next few years. What is clear is that new initiatives that require fast-track authority will be impossible in Washington. Whatever the hopes and ambitions of the White House in the Miami Summit, they have been stalemated by the partisan nature of the U.S. political process at the end of this century and must await a refocusing sometime in the next by another president, Republican or Democrat.

NOTES

1. David E. Sanger, "Clinton Shelving '98 Trade Bill in Favor of New IMF Funds," *New York Times,* January 28, 1998, p. D8.

2. The Rio Group grew out of the Central American wars of the 1980s. In 1983, four states—Mexico, Venezuela, Colombia, and Panama—organized the Contadora Group and offered a plan for the negotiated settlement of the conflict. In 1985 Argentina, Brazil, Peru, and Uruguay organized the Contadora Support Group. Joint meetings of the eight were held over the next eighteen months. In December 1986 the foreign ministers of the eight states met in Rio de Janeiro and adopted a declaration creating the Permanent Mechanism of Consultation and Political Coordination, known as the Rio Group. Annual meetings of heads of state began in November 1987. The Rio Group has become an important sounding board within Latin America for joint discussion of a variety of policy issues.

3. Richard E. Feinberg, *Summitry of the Americas: A Progress Report* (Washington, D.C.: Institute for International Economics, 1997), p. 141.

4. Ibid., p. 142.

5. Ibid.

6. Ibid., pp. 142–143.

7. The Ibero-American summits bring together the heads of state of Latin America, Portugal, and Spain. The United States does not participate. The summits

have become a useful way to reinforce historical ties with the original settlers of the region. They also provide a mechanism for informal meetings with President Fidel Castro of Cuba, who participates.

8. The EU and the Rio Group have held regular meetings of consultation over the years. The EU is Mercosur's main trade partner and donor and, over the last two years, has been gaining ground in investment flows, where it ranks second after the United States; the EU and Mercosur have formally agreed to negotiate a free trade agreement. The EU and Mercosur also signed an interregional framework cooperation agreement on December 15, 1995, that provides for broad, comprehensive exchanges in several political and economic policy areas.

9. U.S. Senate Finance Committee, *Senate Finance Committee Holds Hearing on the Nomination of Charlene Barshefsky as U.S. Trade Representative* (Washington, D.C.: Federal Document Clearing House). Transcript, January 29, 1997.

10. Feinberg, *Summitry of the Americas,* p. 195.

11. "Pan-American Free Trade: Slow, but Ahead," *The Economist,* May 24, 1997, p. 35.

12. Geoff Dyer, "Brazil Urges 'Realism' in All-America Trade Talks," *Financial Times,* May 16, 1997, p. 4.

13. For an analysis of the peso crisis, see Riordan Roett, ed., *The Mexican Peso Crisis: International Perspectives* (Boulder, Colo.: Lynne Rienner, 1996).

14. Feinberg, *Summitry of the Americas,* p. 177.

15. Ibid.

16. Anthony Faiola, "Chile Takes Its Trade Elsewhere," *Washington Post,* December 25, 1997, p. A29.

17. Ibid.

18. David E. Sanger, "Clinton Embarks on a NAFTA Quest," *New York Times,* September 9, 1997, pp. A1, A6.

19. All dollar amounts are U.S. dollars. "Washington Wire: Costly Track," *The Wall Street Journal,* November 7, 1997, p. A1.

20. Anthony Faiola, "Fast-Track Fallout Blankets S. America: Region Skeptical Clinton Can Fulfill Vow to Establish Free-Trade Zone," *Washington Post,* November 12, 1997, p. A4.

21. Raymond Colitt, "S. American Nations in New Drive to Form Trade Pact," *Financial Times,* November 10, 1997, p. 20.

Acronyms

AC	Andean Community
AFL-CIO	American Federation of Labor–Congress of Industrial Organizations
ALADI	Latin American Integration Association (Asociación Latinoamericana de Integración)
ASEAN	Association of Southeast Asian Nations
CET	common external tariff
CMC	Common Market Council
EC	European Community
EU	European Union
Fonplata	Financial Fund for the Development of the River Plate Basin
FTA	free trade agreement
FTAA	Free Trade Area of the Americas
GATT	General Agreement on Tariffs and Trade
GDP	gross domestic product
GMC	Common Market Group (Grupo Mercado Común)
IMF	International Monetary Fund
LAFTA	Latin American Free Trade Association
Mercosul	Portuguese version of Mercosur
Mercosur	Common Market of the South (Mercado Común del Sur)
NAFTA	North American Free Trade Agreement
NATO	North Atlantic Treaty Organization
NTB	nontariff barrier
NTM	New Transatlantic Marketplace

PAC	political action committee
PICE	Program for Integration and Economic Cooperation
R&D	research and development
SAFTA	South American Free Trade Area
SITC	Standard International Trade Classification
UNSC	United Nations Security Council
USTR	U.S. Trade Representative
WTO	World Trade Organization
YPF	Fiscal Oil Fields (Yacimientos Petrolíferos Fiscales)

Bibliography

Agosín, Manuel, and Roberto Alvarez. "La asociación entre Chile y el Mercosur: Costos y beneficios de un año de funcionamiento." *Informe Mercosur* 3 (July–December 1997): appendix. (Buenos Aires, Inter-American Development Bank/Institute for the Integration of Latin America and the Caribbean).

Bataller M., Francisco. "The Relations Between the European Union and Mercosur: Policies, Achievements and Prospects." *EU/LDC News* 3 (December 1996).

Bekerman, Marta, and Pablo Sirlin. "Patrón de especialización y política comercial en la Argentina de los 90." *Desarrollo Económico* 36 (1996) (Buenos Aires).

———. "Los desafíos de la política industrial en el Mercosur." *Revista del Centro de Estudios Bonaerenses* 63-64 (February–March 1997).

Bosco Machado, João, and Ricardo Markwald. "Dinâmica recente do processo de integração do Mercosul." Discussion paper 128, Fundação Centro de Estudos do Comércio Exterior, Rio de Janeiro, 1997.

Bouzas, Roberto. "La agenda económica del Mercosur: Desafíos de política a corto y mediano plazo." *Integración y Comercio* (Buenos Aires) (January–April 1996): 64–87.

———. "Las relaciones comerciales Mercosur–Estados Unidos: Elementos para una agenda minilateral." *Serie Documentos de Trabajo* 4 (1994) (Buenos Aires, Instituto del Servicio Exterior de la Nación).

Bouzas, Roberto, and Jaime Ros. "The North-South Variety of Economic Integration: Issues and Prospects for Latin America." In *Economic Integration in the Western Hemisphere,* edited by Roberto Bouzas and Jaime Ros. Notre Dame, Ind.: Notre Dame University Press, 1994.

Cepeda, Horacio. "Un análisis de la composición de las exportaciones argentinas." Working paper, Instituto de Desarrollo Industrial, Buenos Aires, 1997.

Colitt, Raymond. "S. American Nations in New Drive to Form Trade Pact." *Financial Times,* 10 November 1997, 20.

Devlin, Robert. "Em Defesa do Mercosul." *Revista Brasileira de Comércio Exterior* 50 (January–March 1997) (Rio de Janeiro, Fundação Centro de Estudos do Comércio Exterior).

Di Biase, Héctor N. "Acuerdo Mercosur–Unión Europea: El paso a la segunda fase." *Cuaderno de Negocios Internacionales e Integración* (November–December 1996) (Universidad Católica, Montevideo, Uruguay).

Dromi, Roberto, and Carlos Molina del Pozo. *Acuerdo Mercosur Unión Europea.* Madrid: Ediciones Ciudad Argentina, 1996.

Dyer, Geoff. "Brazil Urges 'Realism' in All-America Trade Talks." *Financial Times,* 16 May 1997, 4.

Faiola, Anthony. "Chile Takes Its Trade Elsewhere." *Washington Post,* 25 December 1997, A29.

———. "Fast-Track Fallout Blankets S. America: Region Skeptical Clinton Can Fulfill Vow to Establish Free-Trade Zone." *Washington Post,* 12 November 1997, A4.

Feinberg, Richard E. *Summitry of the Americas: A Progress Report.* Washington, D.C.: Institute for International Economics, 1997.

Garay, Luis Jorge. "Regionalismo abierto e integración en las Américas." In *Regionalización e integración económica: Instituciones y procesos comparados,* edited by Roberto Bouzas. Buenos Aires: Editorial Nuevohacer, 1997.

González Sánchez, Enrique. "El diálogo político de la Unión Europea con países terceros." *Revista de Derecho Comunitario Europeo* 1 (January–June 1997).

Instituto de Relaciones Europeo-Latinoamericanas [IRELA]. *Closer EU Links with Eastern Europe: Implications for Latin America.* Madrid: IRELA, 1997.

Institute for the Integration of Latin America and the Caribbean [INTAL]/Inter-American Development Bank [IDB]. *Informe Mercosur* 2 (January–June 1997). Buenos Aires: INTAL, IDB, 1997.

Inter-American Development Bank [IDB] and Instituto de Relaciones Europeo-Latinoamericanas [IRELA]. *Foreign Direct Investment in Latin America.* Madrid: IDB and IRELA, 1998.

Izam, Miguel. "Evolución, Análisis y Perpectivas del Mercado Común del Sur." Working paper LC/R 1706, Economic Commission on Latin America and the Caribbean, Santiago, Chile, 1997.

Kahler, Miles. "Regionalism and Institutions: A Comparative Perspective." Paper presented at a meeting of the Instituto del Servicio Exterior de la Nación, Buenos Aires, 1996.

Keohane, Robert, and Stanley Hoffman. "Institutional Change in Europe in the 1980s." In *The New European Community,* edited by Robert Keohane and Stanley Hoffman, 1–39. Boulder, Colo.: Westview Press, 1993.

Kosakoff, Bernardo. "Business Strategies and Industrial Adjustments: The Case of Argentina." Working paper 67, Economic Commission on Latin America and the Caribbean, Buenos Aires, 1996.

Kume, Honorio, and Ricardo Markwald. "As Perspectivas do Mercosul: Configuração da Estrutura Produtiva e Convergência Macroeconômica." In *Perspectivas da economía brasileira,* 205–230. Rio de Janeiro: Instituto de Pesquisa Econômica Aplicada, 1994.

Lavagna, Roberto. "Integração Argentina-Brasil: Origem, Resultados e Perspectivas." In *Cone Sul: A Economia Política da Integração,* edited by Pedro da Motta Veiga, 27–60. Rio de Janeiro: Fundação Centro de Estudos do Comércio Exterior, 1991.

Mansfield, Edward D., and Helen V. Milner. "The Political Economy of Regionalism: An Overview." In *The Political Economy of Regionalism,* edited by Edward D. Mansfield and Helen V. Milner, 1–19. New York: Columbia University Press, 1997.

Motta Veiga, Pedro da. "El Mercosur y el proceso de construcción del ALCA." *Integración y Comercio* 1 (Buenos Aires) (September–December 1997).

Motta Veiga, Pedro da, and João Bosco Machado. "A ALCA e a estratégia negociadora brasileira." *Revista Brasileira de Comércio Exterior* 51 (April–June 1997): 33–42. (Rio de Janeiro, Fundação Centro de Estudos do Comércio Exterior).

"Pan-American Free Trade: Slow, but Ahead." *The Economist,* 24 May 1997, 35.

Pavitt, Keith. "Sectoral Patterns of Technical Change: Towards a Taxonomy and a Theory." *Research Policy* 13 (1984): 343–373.

Peña, Félix. "El Mercosur y la Unión Europea: El Camino hacia una Nueva Alianza Interregional." *Anuario de las Relaciones Europeo-Latinoamericanas* (1993): 133–155. (Madrid, Instituto de Relaciones Europeo-Latinoamericanas).

Picerno, Alfredo, and Pablo Gutiérrez. "Notas sobre la convergencia entre el Mercosur y la Unión Europea." Working paper series 77, Centro Latino-americano de Economía Humana, Montevideo, Uruguay, 1997.

Rodríguez Mendoza, Miguel. "Afinal, que Mercosul é este?" *Revista Brasileira de Comércio Exterior* 50 (1996) (Rio de Janeiro, Fundação Centro de Estudos do Comércio Exterior).

Roett, Riordan, ed. *The Mexican Peso Crisis: International Perspectives.* Boulder, Colo.: Lynne Rienner, 1996.

Sanger, David E. "Clinton Embarks on a NAFTA Quest." *New York Times,* 9 September 1997, A1.

———. "Clinton Shelving '98 Trade Bill in Favor of New IMF Funds." *New York Times,* 28 January 1998, D8.

Tavares Araújo, J., Jr., "Desempenho exportador e integração econômica no hemisfério ocidental." *Revista Brasileira do Comércio Exterior* 51 (April–June 1997): 51–59.

U.S. Senate Finance Committee. *Senate Finance Committee Holds Hearing on the Nomination of Charlene Barshefsky as U.S. Trade Representative.* Washington, D.C.: Federal Document Clearing House. Transcript, 29 January 1997.

Utterback, James M., and Albert E. Murray, "The Influence of Defense Procurement and Sponsorship of Research and Development on the Development of the Civilian Electronics Industry." Working paper 77-5, MIT Center for Policy Alternatives, Cambridge, Mass., 1977.

Vargas Garcia, E. "O pensamento dos militares em política internacional." *Revista Brasileira de Política Internacional* 40, no. 1 (January–June 1997): 18–40.

Viner, Jacob. *The Customs Union Issue.* New York: Carnegie Endowment for International Peace, 1950.

World Trade Organization [WTO]. *Focus Newsletter.* Geneva: WTO, 1997.

Yeats, Alexander. "Does Mercosur's Trade Performance Raise Concerns about the Effects of Regional Trade Arrangements?" Policy research working paper 1729, World Bank, Washington, D.C., 1997.

The Contributors

João Bosco Machado is research associate at the Center for International Trade Studies Foundation (FUNCEX) in Rio de Janeiro.

Roberto Bouzas is senior research fellow at the Latin American School of Social Sciences (FLACSO-Argentina) and the National Foreign Service Institute (ISEN). He is also an independent researcher at the National Council of Scientific and Technical Research (CONICET) and professor of international economics at the University of Buenos Aires.

Wolf Grabendorff is the founding director of the Institute for European–Latin American Relations (IRELA) in Madrid. He is also a member of the international editorial advisory committees of the *Anuario de las Relaciones Europeo-Latinoamericanas,* or ARELA (Madrid), the *European Review of Latin American and Caribbean Studies* (Amsterdam), and the *Journal of Latin American Studies* (Cambridge), among other journals.

Monica Hirst is executive director of the Center for Brazilian Studies Foundation in Buenos Aires. She is also a professor in international relations at the Latin American School of Social Sciences (FLACSO-Argentina) and the National Foreign Service Institute (ISEN).

Ricardo Markwald is research associate at the Center for International Trade Studies Foundation (FUNCEX) in Rio de Janeiro.

Pedro da Motta Veiga is president of the Brazilian Association for the Study of Transnational Enterprises and Economic Globalization (SOBEET). He is also a consultant for the Center for International Trade Studies Foundation (FUNCEX) and various other Brazilian and foreign organizations.

Félix Peña is a founding member of the Argentine Council on Foreign

Relations (CARI). When he wrote the chapter for this book he was the executive director of the Europe-Argentina Club, a private institution that promotes closer ties and greater investment between the European Union and Argentina. He is currently undersecretary of trade at the Argentine Ministry of Economic Affairs. He has also served as undersecretary for hemispheric economic integration in Argentina's Ministry of Foreign Affairs and, as such, was national coordinator for Mercosur negotiations.

Riordan Roett is Sarita and Don Johnston Professor of Political Science and director of the Latin American Studies Program at the Johns Hopkins Paul H. Nitze School of Advanced International Studies (SAIS) in Washington, D.C. He is also founding director of the SAIS Center of Brazilian Studies and the SAIS Program on U.S.-Mexican Relations.

Lia Valls Pereira is director of the Center for Economic and Government Studies at the Getulio Vargas Foundation in Rio de Janeiro.

Index

Abdenur, Roberto, 114, 115
AC. *See* Andean Community
Advisory Forum on Economic and
    Social Matters, 11
Agenda 2000, 14, 15
Agricultural products, 66(table), 68, 69,
    83, 84, 85, 88, 90
ALADI. *See* Latin American Integration
    Association
American Federation of
    Labor–Congress of Industrial
    Organizations (AFL-CIO), 120, 121
Andean Community (AC), 18, 57, 83,
    84–85, 92(nn 8, 9, 10), 123
Antidumping mechanisms, 13, 28
Araújo, Jr., J. Tavares, 27
Argentina, 1, 10, 85, 123(n2); and
    ALADI trade, 82, 92(n3); and Chile,
    83; economic growth rate of, 13, 64;
    energy products of, 69; exports from,
    18, 66–67(tables), 69; foreign policy
    of, 35–36, 37–38, 41–44, 45; GDP
    in, 22(n13); and hemispheric free
    trade, 38, 39, 86, 87; industrial poli-
    cy of, 11, 74; in Mercosur transition
    period, 11, 12, 13, 21(nn 5, 9); post–
    Cold War, 37–38; and security, 38,
    41; and United States, 37, 38, 41, 42,
    43, 44, 47(n5). *See also* Argentine-
    Brazilian relations
Argentine-Brazilian relations, 1, 3, 8–9,
    41–46; Cold War, 36; economic, 13,
    36, 38; and foreign policies, 36,
    41–44, 45; and Mercosur consolida-
    tion, 38–41, 53–54, 56; and relative
    power, 13, 42, 43, 46, 74, 76, 78; and
    security, 3, 43–44; and trade, 9, 13,

23(n28), 31, 42–43, 69. *See also*
    individual countries
Asia, 65, 66–67(tables), 68, 72(table),
    102(tables)
Asunción, Treaty of (1991), 1–2, 9, 38;
    annexes of, 10, 21(n6); provisions
    of, 10–11, 21(n4), 55, 78, 82
Asymmetries, 20, 50, 51, 52, 59, 88–89;
    Argentine-Brazilian, 13, 42, 43, 46,
    74, 76, 78; EU-Mercosur, 98
Automotive sector, 12, 15, 22(n17), 28,
    59, 64, 86

Barshefsky, Charlene, 116
Belo Horizonte ministerial meeting, 57,
    86, 105, 117
Biregional relations, 95–96. *See also*
    Interregional associations
Bolivia, 2, 5(n2), 83–84
Bosco Machado, J., 31
Bouzas, Roberto, 13
Brazil, 1, 10, 42, 43, 46, 123(n2); and
    ALADI trade, 92(n4); domestic poli-
    cy of, 27–29, 30; economic growth
    rate of, 13, 64; exports from, 18,
    22(n15), 26, 28, 30–31,
    66–67(tables); foreign policy of,
    35–36, 37–38, 41, 112, 114; GDP in,
    22(n13), 25; and hemispheric free
    trade, 26, 32, 39, 85–86; imports to,
    26, 28, 30, 31; industrial policy of,
    26, 27, 28–29, 31, 74; investment in,
    28, 31; in Mercosur integration peri-
    od, 11, 12, 13, 14, 15, 16, 21(nn
    5, 9), 23(n23); and Mercosur negoti-
    ations, 25–29, 30–32, 86, 92(n10),
    112; post–Cold War, 37–38; and

133

Free Trade Area of the Americas
(FTAA), 2, 3, 46; and Argentina, 38,
39; and Brazil, 26, 32, 39; and EU-
Mercosur, 39, 56, 57, 107; negotia-
tions for, 15, 19, 22(n20), 23(n26),
87–89, 90–91; and U.S., 15, 22(n20),
87–88, 96, 111, 117
Free trade zones, 51, 52. *See also* Free
Trade Area of the Americas;
Hemispheric free trade
Frei, Eduardo, 118
FTAA. *See* Free Trade Area of the
Americas
Fuel exports, 69

Gaddis, John Lewis, 45
GDP. *See* Gross domestic product
Gephardt, Richard, 120, 121
Gingrich, Newt, 121
Global integration, 18, 54, 64, 70,
79(n4)
GMC. *See* Common Market Group
Gross domestic product (GDP), 7,
22(n13), 25

Hemispheric free trade, 2, 23(n25), 54,
55, 56, 57, 58, 86–87, 113
Historic patrimony, 85, 92(n9)
Hoffman, Stanley, 45
Human rights, 97

Ibero-American summits, 115, 123,
123(n7)
IMF. *See* International Monetary Fund
Imports, 7, 14, 63–64, 99; quotas on,
28. *See also* Tariffs; *under* Brazil;
European Union
Import substitution, 8
Industrialized products, 64, 65,
66(table), 90; and intraindustry
trade, 70, 71–73(table), 80(n8);
labor-intensive, 65, 66(table), 68, 69;
technological intensity of, 65,
67(table), 68, 69. *See also* Product
specialization; Sensitive products
Industrial policy, 2, 74–79, 90. *See also*
under Argentina; Brazil
Infrastructure, 43, 55, 78, 83, 99
Innovation, 76, 77
Insulza, José Miguel, 123
Integration. *See* Voluntary economic
integration

Integration and Economic Cooperation,
Program for (PICE), 9, 36
Integration, Cooperation, and
Development, Treaty on (1988), 9,
21(n3), 36–37
Interdependence, economic, 45, 51–52,
55, 56, 63, 91
International credibility, 37, 38
International economy. *See* Global inte-
gration
International Monetary Fund (IMF), 113
Interregional associations, 106–108. *See*
also Biregional relations
Investment, foreign, 2, 7, 12, 22(n11),
55, 56, 57, 77, 78, 90, 98(tables). *See*
also under Brazil; European Union
Itamarati, 112, 114, 115

Japan, 102(tables)
Joint Parliamentary Commission, 11

Kantor, Mickey, 118
Keohane, Robert, 45

Labor-intensive industry, 65, 66(table),
68, 69
Labor standards, 93(n14), 118, 119, 120
LAFTA. *See* Latin American Free Trade
Association
Lampreia, Luiz Felipe, 117
Las Leñas, Act of (1992), 27
Las Leñas Summit, 56
Latin American Free Trade Association
(LAFTA), 1, 8, 52
Latin American Integration Association
(ALADI), 1, 8, 18, 22(n18), 23(n24),
52, 53, 55, 60, 81, 82, 85, 91(nn 1,
2), 92(n4); exports to, 18, 65,
66–67(tables), 68, 69, 82, 92(n3);
and intraindustry trade, 70, 71(table)
Liberalization. *See* Trade liberalization

Macroeconomic stability. *See*
Stabilization plans
Manufactured products, 31, 65,
66(table), 68, 69, 70, 71–73(table)
Markwald, Ricardo, 31
Mechanical equipment, 31, 70,
71–73(table)
Mediterranean region, 107
Medium-size enterprises, 30, 99
Menem, Carlos, 56

Protocol on Promotion of Investments
from States Not Members of
Mercosur (1994), 12
Public opinion, 55

R&D. *See* Research and development
Redistributive mechanisms, 89
Regionalism, 20, 36, 40, 55
Research and development (R&D), 65,
68, 76, 77
Rio Declaration (1997), 3, 41
Rio Group, 114, 115, 123(n2), 124(n8)
Rome, Treaty of (1957), 16
Rules of origin, 10, 21(n6), 51, 84–85,
92(n8)

Safeguard clauses, 13, 14
SAFTA. *See* South American Free Trade
Area
Salinas de Gortari, Carlos, 112
San Luis presidential summit (1996),
41–42
Santiago Summit (1998), 2, 15, 86,
111
Sectoral agreements, 9, 10
Security, 3, 36, 37, 38, 41, 44, 46(n1)
Sensitive products, 10, 12, 84, 85,
92(n9), 99, 105
Sensitive technology, 37, 38, 41
Services sector, 31, 58, 105
Small enterprises, 30, 99
South American Free Trade Area
(SAFTA), 15, 84, 107
Stabilization plans, 7, 13, 14, 16–17, 78,
89; in Brazil, 16, 23(n23), 28
State intervention, 74, 75, 77
Subsidies, 28, 59, 88
Sugar industry, 12, 59
Summit of the Americas, 2, 3. *See also*
Miami Summit; Santiago Summit
Supranationalism, 11, 20–21, 115

Tariffs, 22(n18); common external, 10,
12, 27, 28, 51, 53, 55, 56, 57, 61(n1),
81; exemptions from, 10, 11, 12,
21(nn 5, 9), 23(n23), 84, 91; reductions in, 10, 12, 15, 82, 83, 92(n6);
zero, 11–12, 53, 54, 61(n1). *See also*
Preferential treatment
Taxation, 28

Technical committees, 11, 21(n8)
Technical education, 76
Technology, 58, 76–78; sensitive, 37,
38, 41. *See also* Industrialized prod-
ucts, technological intensity of
Telecommunications sector, 11, 12, 28,
55, 86
Tella, Guido di, 117
Tequila effect, 3
Trade, Commission on, 11
Trade, intraindustry. *See* Industrialized
products, and intraindustry trade
Trade creation/diversion, 75
Trade liberalization, 8, 9, 10, 18,
23(n25), 27, 28, 29, 55, 89
Transportation sector, 55, 70,
71–73(table), 78

Unfair trade practices, 59
United Nations peacekeeping, 41, 44
United Nations Security Council membership, 3, 42, 43
United States, 37, 38, 39, 77, 96,
106–107; and Argentina, 37, 38, 41,
42, 43, 44, 47(n5); and Brazil, 37,
41, 42, 86–87, 111–112, 113–115,
116–117; domestic politics of,
112–113, 118, 119–123; and FTAA,
15, 22(n20), 87–88, 96, 111, 117;
investment of, 102(tables); and
Mercosur, 96, 116–117; and Mexico,
112. *See also* Fast-track authority;
Hemispheric free trade
Uruguay, 1, 9, 10, 12, 18, 21(nn 5, 9),
35, 44, 85, 123(n2)

Values discussions, 97
Venezuela, 40, 85, 92(n10), 123(n2)
Voluntary economic integration, 50–52,
59, 97; broadening-deepening of,
49–52, 106–107. *See also* Biregional
relations; Interregional associations

Wage differential, 120
World Bank, 64
World Trade Organization (WTO), 14,
58, 64, 87–88, 93(n13)

Yeats, Alexander, 64, 69
YPF. *See* Fiscal Oil Fields